QUOTABLE WISDOM

WISDOM

•

Barack Obama

QUOTABLE WISDOM

·

Barack Obama

EDITED BY CAROL KELLY-GANGI

STERLING
New York

STERLING
New York

An Imprint of Sterling Publishing Co., Inc.
1166 Avenue of the Americas
New York, NY 10036

This Sterling edition published in 2017
Previously published in 2016 as *Barack Obama: His Essential Wisdom*
© 2016 Sterling Publishing Co., Inc.

ISBN 978-1-4549-2835-5

Distributed in Canada by Sterling Publishing Co., Inc.
c/o Canadian Manda Group, 664 Annette Street Toronto, Ontario, Canada M6S 2C8
Distributed in the United Kingdom by GMC Distribution Services
Castle Place, 166 High Street, Lewes, East Sussex, England BN7 1XU
Distributed in Australia by NewSouth Books
45 Beach Street, Coogee, NSW 2034, Australia

For information about custom editions, special sales, and premium
and corporate purchases, please contact Sterling Special Sales at
800-805-5489 or specialsales@sterlingpublishing.com.

Manufactured in the United States of America

2 4 6 8 10 9 7 5 3 1

sterlingpublishing.com

Book design by Christine Heun

Photo Credits
Alamy: DOD Photo: 108; © Angus Lamond: 62; NG Images: 14;
Reuters: 22, 80; White House Photo: cover, 50, 68; Z2A1: 92

Getty Images: © Barcroft Media: 74; © Brooks Kraft

LLC/Corbis: x; © Saul Loeb/AFP: 56; © Scott Olson: 6; © Pete Souza/
Chicago Tribune/MCT: 44; © Mario Tama: 36

WhiteHouse.gov: 114; Official White House Photo by Pete Souza: 28,
86, 102, 122, 126, 132

CONTENTS

Introduction vii

Early Years 1
America 7
Politics 15
The 2008 Presidential Election 23
The Presidency 29
Government, Democracy, and Freedom 37
Equality and Justice 45
The Economy, Labor, and Business 51
Gun Violence and Crime 57
Reform and Accomplishments 63
Race and Racism 69
Women 75
The Environment 81
Knowledge, Education, and Innovation 87
Peace, War, and Foreign Policy 93
Hardship, Hope, and Change 103
Religion, Morality, and Values 109
Family 115
Life's Pleasures 123
Presidential Wit 127
The Wisdom of Barack Obama 133

Chronology 138

To my family,
John, John Christopher, and Emily Grace,
with a heart full of love

INTRODUCTION

America is not the project of any one person. Because the single-most powerful word in our democracy is the word "We." "We The People." "We Shall Overcome." "Yes We Can." That word is owned by no one. It belongs to everyone. Oh, what a glorious task we are given, to continually try to improve this great nation of ours.

—Fiftieth anniversary of the Selma-to-Montgomery marches,
Edmund Pettus Bridge, Selma, Alabama, March 7, 2015

Barack Obama was still in the White House when historians began the debating where his presidency would rank among his 43 counterparts—even though history suggests it will take decades to achieve clarity and consensus. Even now at the end of his second term in office, historians can already point to key achievements of President Obama's tenure that will factor into any discussion of his legacy: the Affordable Care Act; the economic recovery program; his bold leadership on climate change; ending the war in Iraq; the killing of Osama bin Laden; and his decisive actions on prison reform and same-sex marriage equality.

Of course, President Obama's unlikely rise to the Oval Office as the first African-American president is well known. He is the son of a Kenyan father who was largely absent from his life, and a single mother, who, along with her devoted parents, raised him with a strong set of family values, dedication to hard work and service, and the belief that every American deserves a fair shot at the American Dream.

Even before Barack Obama began his meteoric rise in American politics, he was able to captivate audiences with the power of his words. He published a bestselling memoir, *Dreams of My Father*, in 1995, one year before being elected to his first office, in the Illinois Senate. His speech at the 2004 Democratic National Convention was hailed as one of the finest pieces of political rhetoric in modern American history. And throughout his presidency, his words of hope and optimism proved both inspirational and healing to the country in good times and bad.

Barack Obama: Quotable Wisdom gathers more than 300 memorable quotations from the 44th President of the United States. The selections have been carefully curated from his speeches, conferences, summits, town hall meetings, as well as from his interviews, essays, books, tweets, social media posts, and other writings over the course of the past twenty years. Arranged thematically, the excerpts reveal the great intellect, passionate views, and steadfast determination that have marked President Obama's public life.

In the selections, he vividly expresses his belief in America, in the pursuit of the American Dream, and in the core values that make us who we are. He speaks passionately about the need for hope in the face of hardship; the on-going quest for equality and inclusion; and the pursuit of even-handed justice in order to fulfill the promises set forth by our Founders. He shares his fervent belief in protecting our environment and in leading the way on climate change. And he tirelessly sets forth the need for gun reform, as he poignantly expresses his grief at the staggering number of American lives cut short by gun violence. Elsewhere, President Obama imparts his pragmatic wisdom on such topics as growing the economy;

improving education; leading the way in innovation; and striving for peace in the world.

In other excerpts, we see a more personal side of President Obama. He lovingly recalls his mother and the life lessons she taught him with words and deed. Other selections reveal his devotion to his wife Michelle, and the pride and joy he feels for his daughters Malia and Sasha. He shares insights from his own spiritual journey and what drew him to his Christian faith. On a lighter note, one chapter touches on the President's comedic side—from roasting fellow politicians to trading barbs with sports figures. The final chapter is a sampling of the President's musings on such subjects as the path to success; the meaning of compromise; and the value of the arts.

Barack Obama: Quotable Wisdom invites readers to experience the powerful words of our 44th president—words that galvanized a nation to hold onto hope and believe in change.

—CAROL KELLY-GANGI,
2016

EARLY YEARS

I know that she was the kindest, most generous spirit I have ever known, and that what is best in me I owe to her.

—*Referring to his mother,* Dreams from My Father:
A Story of Race and Inheritance

• ◆ •

You know, I was born to a teenage mother. My father left when I was two. So I was raised by a single mom and my grandparents. And they didn't have money, and they didn't have fame. What they could give me was love, they gave me an education, and they gave me hope.

—*Campaign speech to supporters after winning Wisconsin primary,
Houston, February 19, 2008*

• ◆ •

I grew up in Hawaii, and had two wonderful grandparents from Kansas who poured everything they had into helping my mother raise my sister and me—who worked with her to teach us about love and respect and the obligations we have to one another.

—*Father's Day speech, Apostolic Church of God, Chicago, June 15, 2008*

• ◆ •

I had a heroic mom and wonderful grandparents who helped raise me and my sister, and it's because of them that I'm able to stand here today. But despite all their extraordinary love and attention, that doesn't mean that I didn't feel my father's absence. That's something that leaves a hole in a child's heart that a government can't fill.

—*Young Men's Barbeque, White House, Washington, D.C., June 19, 2009*

• ◆ •

There was only one problem: my father was missing. He had left paradise, and nothing that my mother or grandparents told me could obviate that single, unassailable fact.

—Dreams from My Father: A Story of Race and Inheritance

Growing up, I absorbed a lot of negative stereotypes about how I should behave as a black teenager and fell into some of the same traps that a lot of black male youth do. It wasn't preordained that I would go to Columbia or to Harvard. I didn't have a father in the house, which meant that I didn't have a lot of role models in terms of how I should operate.

—Interview, Chicago Sun-Times, *June 26, 2005*

• ◆ •

As a teen, I had this divided identity—one inside the home, one for the outside world. It wasn't until I got to college that I started realizing that was fundamentally dishonest. I knew there had to be a different way for me to understand myself as a black man and yet not reject the love and values given to me by my mother and her parents. I had to reconcile that I could be proud of my African-American heritage and yet not be limited by it.

—Interview, O, the Oprah Magazine, *November 2004*

• ◆ •

The opportunity that Hawaii offered—to experience a variety of cultures in a climate of mutual respect—became an integral part of my world view, and a basis for the values that I hold most dear.

—Essay, Punahou Bulletin, *1999*

• ◆ •

Well, at fifteen, I would have told myself, "Hit the books and stop goofing off." Because at fifteen, I was not the most responsible young man. I loved basketball, but outside of basketball, I was, I was getting by on my charm and wit, but not taking my schoolwork as seriously as I could have.

—Video interview with baseball player Derek Jeter,
The Players' Tribune, *June 22, 2016*

I had people who encouraged me—not just my mom and grandparents, but wonderful teachers and community leaders—and they'd push me to work hard and study hard and make the most of myself. And if I didn't listen they said it again. And if I didn't listen they said it a third time. And they would give me second chances, and third chances. They never gave up on me, and so I didn't give up on myself.

—Announcing "My Brother's Keeper" initiative, White House East Room, Washington, D.C., February 27, 2014

At the time of his death, my father remained a myth to me, both more and less than a man.

—Dreams from My Father: A Story of Race and Inheritance

I have been chasing this same goal my entire adult career, and that is creating an America that is fairer, more compassionate and has greater understanding between its various peoples.

—Interview, Chicago Tribune, March 18, 2004

She is the smartest, toughest, funniest, best friend that I could ever hope for, and she's always had my back.

—Referring to wife, Michelle Obama, Washington Post, December 11, 2006

I moved to Illinois over two decades ago. I was a young man then, just a year out of college; I knew no one in Chicago, was without money or family connections. But a group of churches had offered me a job as a community organizer for $13,000 a year. And I accepted the job, sight unseen, motivated then by a single, simple, powerful idea—that I might play a small part in building a better America.

—Declaring presidential candidacy, Springfield, Illinois, February 10, 2007

Some of you know I used to work as a community organizer with churches on the south side of Chicago after the steel plants had laid thousands of people off. And we brought together black and white and Hispanic to try to create job training programs for the unemployed and bring economic development to neighborhoods that had fallen on hard times. And it was the best education I ever had, because it taught me that ordinary people can do extraordinary things when they're given an opportunity.

—Campaign speech to supporters after winning Wisconsin primary, Houston, February 19, 2008

For someone like me, who had barely known his father, who had spent much of his life traveling from place to place, his bloodlines scattered to the four winds, the home that Frasier and Marian Robinson had built for themselves and their children stirred a longing for stability and a sense of place that I had not realized was there.

—The Audacity of Hope

When my daughters were born, I made a pledge to them, and to myself, that I would do everything I could to give them some things I didn't have. And I decided that if I could be one thing in life, it would be to be a good father.

—Fatherhood Town Hall, White House East Room, June 19, 2009

And I would not be standing here tonight without the unyielding support of my best friend for the last 16 years, the rock of our family, the love of my life, the nation's next first lady Michelle Obama.

—Presidential acceptance speech, Grant Park, Chicago, November 4, 2008

AMERICA

My parents shared not only an improbable love; they shared an abiding faith in the possibilities of this nation. They would give me an African name, Barack, or "blessed," believing that in a tolerant America your name is no barrier to success. . . . I stand here today grateful for the diversity of my heritage, aware that my parents' dreams live on in my two precious daughters. I stand here knowing that my story is part of the larger American story, that I owe a debt to all of those who came before me, and that in no other country on Earth is my story even possible.

—Keynote address, Democratic National Convention,
Boston, July 27, 2004

• ◆ •

Now, as a nation, we don't promise equal outcomes, but we were founded on the idea everybody should have an equal opportunity to succeed. No matter who you are, what you look like, where you come from, you can make it. That's an essential promise of America. Where you start should not determine where you end up.

—College Opportunity Summit, Ronald Reagan Building,
Washington, D.C., December 4, 2014

• ◆ •

There's not a liberal America and a conservative America; there's the United States of America. There's not a black America and a white America and Latino America and Asian America; there's the United States of America.

—Keynote address, Democratic National Convention,
Boston, July 27, 2004

My fellow Americans, we are and always will be a nation of immigrants. We were strangers once, too. And whether our forebears were strangers who crossed the Atlantic, or the Pacific, or the Rio Grande, we are here only because this country welcomed them in, and taught them that to be an American is about something more than what we look like, or what our last names are, or how we worship. What makes us Americans is our shared commitment to an ideal—that all of us are created equal, and all of us have the chance to make of our lives what we will.

—Television address on immigration, Washington, D.C., November 20, 2014

• ◆ •

We didn't raise the Statue of Liberty with her back to the world, we did it with her light shining as a beacon to the world. And whether we were Irish or Italians or Germans crossing the Atlantic, or Japanese or Chinese crossing the Pacific; whether we crossed the Rio Grande or flew here from all over the world—generations of immigrants have made this country into what it is. It's what makes us special.

—Outlining immigration reform, Del Sol High School,
Las Vegas, November 21, 2014

• ◆ •

Sixty years ago, when the Russians beat us into space, we didn't deny Sputnik was up there. We didn't argue about the science, or shrink our research and development budget. We built a space program almost overnight. And twelve years later, we were walking on the moon. Now, that spirit of discovery is in our DNA. America is Thomas Edison and the Wright Brothers and George Washington Carver. America is Grace Hopper and Katherine Johnson and Sally Ride. America is every immigrant and entrepreneur from Boston to Austin to Silicon Valley, racing to shape a better world. That's who we are.

—State of the Union Address, Washington, D.C., January 12, 2016

And what the American people hope—what they deserve—is for all of us, Democrats and Republicans, to work through our differences; to overcome the numbing weight of our politics. For while the people who sent us here have different backgrounds, different stories, different beliefs, the anxieties they face are the same. The aspirations they hold are shared: a job that pays the bills; a chance to get ahead; most of all, the ability to give their children a better life.

—*State of the Union Address, Washington, D.C., January 27, 2010*

Never forget that we have it within our power to shape history in this country. It is not in our character to sit idly by as victims of fate or circumstance, for we are a people of action and innovation, forever pushing the boundaries of what's possible.

—Promoting health care alternatives, University of Iowa,
Iowa City, Iowa, May 29, 2007

We believe the little girl who's offered an escape from poverty by a great teacher or a grant for college could become the next Steve Jobs or the scientist who cures cancer or the president of the United States, and it is in our power to give her that chance.

—Acceptance speech for second term, Democratic National Convention,
Charlotte, North Carolina, September 6, 2012

That's the America I know. That's the country we love. Clear-eyed. Big-hearted. Undaunted by challenge. Optimistic that unarmed truth and unconditional love will have the final word. That's what makes me so hopeful about our future. I believe in change because I believe in you, the American people.

—State of the Union Address, Washington, D.C., January 12, 2016

We're not a fragile people. We're not a frightful people. Our power doesn't come from some self-declared savior promising that he alone can restore order as long as we do things his way. We don't look to be ruled. Our power comes from those immortal declarations first put to paper right here in Philadelphia all those years ago: We hold these truths to be self-evident, that all men are created equal; that We the People, can form a more perfect union.

—Endorsing Hillary Clinton as presidential nominee, Democratic National
Convention, Philadelphia, July 27, 2016

We are big and vast and diverse; a nation of people with different backgrounds and beliefs, different experiences and stories, but bound by our shared ideal that no matter who you are or what you look like, how you started off, or how and who you love, America is a place where you can write your own destiny. We are a people who believe that every single child is entitled to life and liberty and the pursuit of happiness.

—*Commending the Supreme Court decision on marriage equality,*
White House Rose Garden, June 26, 2015

It's young people like that that keep me going—folks who prove that Immigrants aren't somehow changing the American character; immigrants are the American character. That's who we are. It's the DREAMers full of optimism. The moms and dads working long hours to give their kids a better shot. The entrepreneurs who came here to start new businesses and put Americans to work. The teachers and the nurses and the lawyers who wake up at the crack of dawn to get ahead. And the folks who clean up after us. And the folks who care for our grandparents. The folks who are so proud of this country that they carry a pocket Constitution in their breast pocket.

—*39th Annual Congressional Hispanic Caucus Institute Gala,*
Washington, D.C., September 15, 2016

America is not the project of any one person. Because the single-most powerful word in our democracy is the word "We." "We the People." "We Shall Overcome." "Yes We Can." That word is owned by no one. It belongs to everyone. Oh, what a glorious task we are given, to continually try to improve this great nation of ours.

—*Fiftieth anniversary of the Selma-to-Montgomery marches,*
Edmund Pettus Bridge, Selma, Alabama, March 7, 2015

America has changed over the years. But these values that my grandparents taught me—they haven't gone anywhere. They're as strong as ever, still cherished by people of every party, every race, every faith. They live on in each of us. . . . That's why anyone who threatens our values, whether fascists or communists or jihadists or homegrown demagogues, will always fail in the end. That is America. That is America. Those bonds of affection; that common creed. We don't fear the future; we shape it. We embrace it, as one people, stronger together than we are on our own.

—Endorsing Hillary Clinton as presidential nominee, Democratic National Convention, Philadelphia, July 27, 2016

POLITICS

Politics depends on our ability to persuade each other of common aims based on a common reality. It involves the compromise, the art of what's possible.

> —*Keynote address, "A Call to Renewal," Building a Covenant for a New America conference, Washington, D.C., June 28, 2006*

• ◆ •

The point is, politics has never been for the thin-skinned or the faint of heart, and if you enter the arena, you should expect to get roughed up. Moreover, Democracy in a nation of more than 300 million people is inherently difficult.

> —*Commencement address, University of Michigan, Ann Arbor, Michigan, May 1, 2010*

• ◆ •

Those of us who have the privilege to serve this country have an obligation to do our job as best we can. We come from different parties, but we are Americans first. And that's why disagreement cannot mean dysfunction. It can't degenerate into hatred. The American people's hopes and dreams are what matters, not ours. Our obligations are to them.

> —*Announcing reopening of the federal government after sixteen-day government shutdown, White House State Dining Room, October 17, 2013*

• ◆ •

I think the biggest mistake politicians make is being inauthentic. By writing about my mistakes, I was trying to show how I was vulnerable to the same pitfalls as American youth everywhere.

> —*Interview,* O, the Oprah Magazine, *November 2004*

When I speak, the first thing I confront is people's cynicism.
I understand it. It seems like politics is a business and not
a mission . . . . But the civil rights movement was a political
movement. The movement to give women the vote was political.
We are all connected as one people, and our mutual obligations
have to express themselves not only in our families, not only in
our churches, not only in our synagogues and mosques, but in our
government, too.

—*Interview,* O, the Oprah Magazine, *November 2004*

• ✦ •

I am surprised at how many elected officials—even the good ones—
spend so much time talking about the mechanics of politics and
not matters of substance. They have this poker chip mentality, this
overriding interest in retaining their seats or in moving their careers
forward, and the business and game of politics, the political horse
race, is all they talk about.

—*Interview,* Chicago Reader, *December 8, 1995*

• ✦ •

To me, the issue is not are you centrist or are you liberal? The issue
to me is, Is what you're proposing going to work? Can you build a
working coalition to make the lives of people better? And if it can
work, you should support it whether it's centrist, conservative, or
liberal.

—*Interview,* New York Magazine, *October 2, 2006*

A good compromise, a good piece of legislation, is like a good sentence. Or a good piece of music. Everybody can recognize it. They say, "Huh. It works. It makes sense."

—Interview, New Yorker, *May 31, 2004*

⋅◆⋅

Well, the time for bickering is over. The time for games has passed. Now is the season for action. Now is when we must bring the best ideas of both parties together, and show the American people that we can still do what we were sent here to do.

—Address to Joint Session of Congress on Health Care,
Washington, D.C., September 9, 2009

⋅◆⋅

You want everybody to act like adults, quit playing games, realize it's not just "My way or the highway."

—Remarks to the press after late-night meeting with members of
Congress about reaching a budget resolution to prevent a
government shutdown, White House, April 6, 2011

⋅◆⋅

I have a better idea: Do something, Congress. Do anything to help working Americans.

—Weekly address, White House, July 12, 2014

⋅◆⋅

After more than 100 days, the Supreme Court still needs its 9th judge, but the Senate GOP refuses to do its job and consider Judge Garland.

—@POTUS, Twitter, June 30, 2016

And I believe that our politics—when our politics are at our best—is not based on identity politics, but it's based on a sense that everybody should have a fair shot and everybody should get a fair shake.

—Interview, National Public Radio, July 1, 2016

· ◆ ·

We need leaders in Congress who know the American Dream is not something that a wall can contain.

—Hillary Clinton rally, Philadelphia, September 13, 2016

· ◆ ·

Our country's better off when the Democratic nominee for the presidency and the Republican nominee are both qualified to be president and can be effective because you never know what happens. I'm a Democrat, I prefer Democratic policies. But I want a serious Republican party and serious Republican nominees.

—Interview, BuzzFeed, May 16, 2015

· ◆ ·

But this will be an election like every other election. And I think all of us at some points in our lives have played sports or maybe just played in a schoolyard or a sandbox. And sometimes folks, if they lose, they start complaining that they got cheated. But I've never heard of somebody complaining about being cheated before the game was over, or before the score is even tallied.

—Responding to question about presidential candidate Donald Trump's claims that the 2016 presidential election will be "rigged" against him, press conference, August 4, 2016

· ◆ ·

What Washington needs is adult supervision.

—Fundraising letter, October 2006

My theme will be that the Democratic Party has always stood for giving everyone an equal chance, despite the circumstances of their birth. My story is emblematic of that . . .

—Explaining content of his forthcoming speech, Democratic National Convention, Boston, July 26, 2004 (as reported in National Review, *July 27, 2004)*

· ◆ ·

But we can't expect to solve our problems if all we do is tear each other down. You can disagree with a certain policy without demonizing the person who espouses it. You can question somebody's views and their judgment without questioning their motives or their patriotism. . . . The problem is that this kind of vilification and over-the-top rhetoric closes the door to the possibility of compromise. It undermines democratic deliberation. . . . It makes it nearly impossible for people who have legitimate but bridgeable differences to sit down at the same table and hash things out. It robs us of a rational and serious debate, the one we need to have about the very real and very big challenges facing this nation. It coarsens our culture, and at its worst, it can send signals to the most extreme elements of our society that perhaps violence is a justifiable response.

—Commencement address, University of Michigan, Ann Arbor, Michigan, May 1, 2010

· ◆ ·

Have principles and issues you are passionate about, and act; worry more about doing something than being something.

—Responding to Twitter questioner @FieldEmma47, who sought advice for an aspiring politician, @POTUS, Twitter, July 1, 2015

I found during the course of my political career on the national scene—which is relatively compressed compared to some of these other presidents—there's a point where the vanity burns away and you've had your fill of your name in the papers, or big adoring crowds, or the exercise of power. And for me that happened fairly quickly. And then you are really focused on: What am I going to get done with this strange privilege that's been granted to me? How do I make myself worthy of it?

—*Interview with Doris Kearns Goodwin,* Vanity Fair, *November 2016*

THE 2008 PRESIDENTIAL ELECTION

In a country of 300 million people, there is a certain degree of audacity required for anybody to say, "I'm the best person to lead this country."

—Interview, Associated Press, November 2006

. ◆ .

I recognize there is a certain presumptuousness in this, a certain audacity, to this announcement. I know that I haven't spent a lot of time learning the ways of Washington, but I've been there long enough to know that the ways of Washington must change. People who love their country can change it.

—Declaring his presidential candidacy, Springfield, Illinois, February 10, 2007

. ◆ .

But the decision to run for president is a very serious one. And it's a very humbling decision. I have to feel that I have something unique to offer the country that no other person can provide right now.

—Interview, Ebony, February 2007

. ◆ .

But the life of a tall, gangly, self-made Springfield lawyer tells us that a different future is possible. He tells us that there is power in words. He tells us that there is power in conviction. That beneath all the differences of race and religion, faith and station, we are one people. He tells us that there is power in hope.

—Declaring his presidential candidacy, Springfield, Illinois, February 10, 2007

. ◆ .

But above all, I will never forget who this victory truly belongs to. It belongs to you.

*—Presidential acceptance speech, Grant Park,
Chicago, November 4, 2008*

But we always knew that hope is not blind optimism. It's not ignoring the enormity of the task ahead or the roadblocks that stand in our path. It's not sitting on the sidelines or shirking from a fight. Hope is that thing inside us that insists, despite all the evidence to the contrary, that something better awaits us if we have the courage to reach for it, and to work for it, and to fight for it.

—Campaign speech to supporters after Iowa Caucus,
Des Moines, Iowa, January 3, 2008

You, all of you who are here tonight, all who put so much heart and soul and work into this campaign, you can be the new majority who can lead this nation out of a long political darkness. Democrats, independents, and Republicans who are tired of the division and distraction that has clouded Washington, who know that we can disagree without being disagreeable, who understand that if we mobilize our voices to challenge the money and influence that stood in our way and challenge ourselves to reach for something better, there's no problem we can't solve, there is no destiny we cannot fulfill.

—Campaign speech to supporters after New Hampshire
primary, January 8, 2008

We know that what began as a whisper has now swelled to a chorus that cannot be ignored, that will not be deterred, that will ring out across this land as a hymn that will heal this nation, repair this world, make this time different than all the rest. Yes, we can.

—Campaign speech, Chicago, February 5, 2008

Now, we need a president who sees government, not as a tool to enrich friends and high-priced lobbyists, but as the defender of fairness and opportunity for every American. That's what this country has always been about, and that's the kind of president I'll be.

—Various speeches, including Manchester, New Hampshire, June 22, 2007

. ◆ .

For decades we've had politicians in Washington who talk about family values, but we haven't had policies that value families. Instead, it's harder for working parents to make a living while raising their kids. And we know that the system is especially stacked against women, and that's why Washington has to change.

—"Change that Works for You" discussion with working women, Flying Star Café, Albuquerque, New Mexico, June 23, 2008

. ◆ .

If we think that we can secure our country by just talking tough without acting tough and smart, then we will misunderstand this moment and miss its opportunities. If we think that we can use the same partisan playbook where we just challenge our opponent's patriotism to win an election, then the American people will lose. The times are too serious for this kind of politics.

—Veterans of Foreign Wars Convention, Orlando, Florida, August 19, 2008

. ◆ .

That's not change. That's just calling the same thing something different. But you can put lipstick on a pig—it's still a pig. You can wrap an old fish in a piece of paper called change; it's still going to stink after eight years. We've had enough of the same old thing.

—Campaign speech referencing Sarah Palin's comments about lipstick, pit bulls, and hockey moms, Lebanon, Virginia, September 9, 2008

If John McCain wants to have a debate about who has the temperament and judgment to serve as the next commander-in-chief, that's a debate I'm ready to have.

—*Accepting Democratic presidential nomination, Democratic National Convention, Denver, August 28, 2008*

• ◆ •

I know these are difficult times. I know folks are worried. But I also know that now is not the time for fear or panic. Now is the time for resolve and steady leadership. Because I know we can steer ourselves out of this crisis. This is a nation that has faced down war and depression, great challenges and great threats. We have seen always that mountaintop from the deepest valley. We have always risen to the moment when the moment was hard—and we can do it again. We can restore confidence in our economy and renew that fundamental belief—that here in America, our destiny is not written for us, but by us.

—*Campaign speech, Philadelphia, October 11, 2008*

THE PRESIDENCY

Tonight we proved once more that the true strength of our nation comes not from the might of our arms or the scale of our wealth, but from the enduring power of our ideals: democracy, liberty, opportunity, and unyielding hope. . . . This is our time, to put our people back to work and open doors of opportunity for our kids; to restore prosperity and promote the cause of peace; to reclaim the American dream and reaffirm that fundamental truth, that, out of many, we are one; that while we breathe, we hope. And where we are met with cynicism and doubts and those who tell us that we can't, we will respond with that timeless creed that sums up the spirit of a people: Yes, we can.

—*Presidential acceptance speech, Grant Park, Chicago, November 4, 2008*

Our challenges may be new. The instruments with which we meet them may be new. But those values upon which our success depends—honesty and hard work, courage and fair play, tolerance and curiosity, loyalty and patriotism—these things are old. These things are true. They have been the quiet force of progress throughout our history.

—*Inaugural Address, Washington, D.C., January 21, 2009*

There is probably a perverse pride in my administration . . . that we were going to do the right thing, even if short-term it was unpopular. And I think anybody who's occupied this office has to remember that success is determined by an intersection in policy and politics and that you can't be neglecting of marketing and P.R. and public opinion.

—*Interview,* New York Times Magazine, *October 12, 2010*

The weight of this crisis will not determine the destiny of this nation. The answers to our problems don't lie beyond our reach. They exist in our laboratories and universities; in our fields and our factories; in the imaginations of our entrepreneurs and the pride of the hardest-working people on Earth. Those qualities that have made America the greatest force of progress and prosperity in human history we still possess in ample measure. What is required now is for this country to pull together, confront boldly the challenges we face, and take responsibility for our future once more.

—*Address to Joint Session of Congress, Washington, D.C., February 24, 2009*

• ◆ •

The one thing I've prided myself on before I was President—and it turns out that continues to be true as President—I'm a persistent son of a gun. I just stay at it. And I'm just gonna keep on staying at it, as long as I'm in this office. And we're gonna get it right. And America will succeed. I am absolutely confident about that.

—*Interview, 60 Minutes, December 9, 2011 (aired December 11, 2011)*

• ◆ •

One year ago, I took office amid two wars, an economy rocked by a severe recession, a financial system on the verge of collapse, and a government deeply in debt. Experts from across the political spectrum warned that if we did not act, we might face a second depression. So we acted—immediately and aggressively. And one year later, the worst of the storm has passed.

—*State of the Union Address, Washington, D.C., January 27, 2010*

. . . [T]he future rewards those who press on. With patient and firm determination, I am going to press on for jobs. I'm going to press on for equality. I'm going to press on for the sake of our children. I'm going to press on for the sake of all those families who are struggling right now. I don't have time to feel sorry for myself. I don't have time to complain. I am going to press on.

—*Congressional Black Caucus Foundation Phoenix Awards Dinner, Washington, D.C., September 24, 2011*

Four years ago, I promised to end the war in Iraq. We did. I promised to refocus on the terrorists who actually attacked us on 9/11. And we have. We've blunted the Taliban's momentum in Afghanistan, and in 2014, our longest war will be over. A new tower rises above the New York skyline; al Qaeda is on the path to defeat; and Osama bin Laden is dead.

—*Accepting nomination for second term, Democratic National Convention, Charlotte, North Carolina, September 6, 2012*

It's one of the few regrets of my presidency—that the rancor and suspicion between the parties has gotten worse instead of better. I have no doubt a president with the gifts of Lincoln or Roosevelt might have better bridged the divide, and I guarantee I'll keep trying to be better so long as I hold this office.

—*State of the Union Address, Washington, D.C., January 12, 2016*

I just want to emphasize the degree to which we are in serious times and this is a really serious job. This is not entertainment. This is not a reality show. This is a contest for the presidency of the United States.

—*Press conference, White House, May 6, 2016*

So what drives me as a grandson, a son, a father—as an American—
is to make sure that every striving, hardworking, optimistic kid in
America has the same incredible chance that this country gave me. . . .
[A]nd for the rest of my presidency, that's where you should expect my
administration to focus all our efforts.

*—Addressing economic mobility, Town Hall Education Arts
Recreation Campus, Washington, D.C., December 4, 2013*

Now, I am going to be working with Congress where I can to
accomplish this [year of action], but I'm also going to act on my
own if Congress is deadlocked. I've got a pen to take executive
actions where Congress won't, and I've got a telephone to rally folks
around the country on this mission.

—College Opportunity Summit, Washington, D.C., January 16, 2014

So part of my job as president is to figure out how I can keep America
safe doing the least damage possible in really tough, bad situations.
And I don't have the luxury of just not doing anything and then being
able to stand back and feel as if my conscience is clear.

*—Discussion with students at University of Chicago
Law School, April 7, 2016*

. . . [E]ight years ago, you may remember Hillary and I were rivals
for the Democratic nomination. We battled for a year and a half.
Let me tell you, it was tough, because Hillary was tough. I was worn
out. She was doing everything I was doing, but just like Ginger
Rogers, it was backwards in heels.

*—Endorsing Hillary Clinton as presidential nominee, Democratic National
Convention, Philadelphia, July 27, 2016*

Those of us who have had the singular privilege to hold the office of the Presidency know well that progress in this country can be hard and it can be slow, frustrating and sometimes you're stymied. The office humbles you. You're reminded daily that in this great democracy, you are but a relay swimmer in the currents of history, bound by decisions made by those who came before, reliant on the efforts of those who will follow to fully vindicate your vision. But the presidency also affords a unique opportunity to bend those currents—by shaping our laws and by shaping our debates; by working within the confines of the world as it is, but also by reimagining the world as it should be.

—Lyndon B. Johnson Presidential Library Civil Rights Summit, Austin, Texas, April 10, 2014

⋅◆⋅

I'm far more mindful of my own failings, knowing exactly what Lincoln meant when he said, "I have been driven to my knees many times by the overwhelming conviction that I had no place else to go."

—Accepting nomination for second term, Democratic National Convention, Charlotte, North Carolina, September 6, 2012

⋅◆⋅

Time and again, you've picked me up. And I hope, sometimes, I picked you up, too. And tonight, I ask you to do for Hillary Clinton what you did for me. I ask you to carry her the same way you carried me. Because you're who I was talking about 12 years ago when I talked about hope. It's been you who fueled my dogged faith in our future, even when the odds were great; even when the road is long. Hope in the face of difficulty. Hope in the face of uncertainty. The audacity of hope.

—Endorsing Hillary Clinton as presidential nominee, Democratic National Convention, Philadelphia, July 27, 2016

Leadership means a wise application of military power, and rallying the world behind causes that are right. It means seeing our foreign assistance as a part of our national security, not something separate, not charity.

—State of the Union Address, Washington, D.C., January 12, 2016

• ◆ •

I think of myself as a relay runner. I take the baton. Sometimes, you take the baton and you're behind in the race, and you've got to run a little bit harder to catch up. Hopefully, by the time you pass on the baton, you're a little bit better positioned in the race. And I think there is a humility that comes out of this office, because you feel that no matter how much you've done, there's more work to do. But I think that there is a confidence that well-meaning people working together can—can change the country for the better. I've seen it happen.

—Interview, National Public Radio, July 1, 2016

• ◆ •

. . . I can say with confidence there has never been a man or a woman—not me, not Bill, nobody—more qualified than Hillary Clinton to serve as president of the United States of America.

—Endorsing Hillary Clinton as presidential nominee, Democratic National Convention, Philadelphia, July 27, 2016

• ◆ •

Every day, the White House receives thousands of letters from Americans across the country. Every night, I read 10 of them. These letters are my chance to hear directly from the people I serve—and it's one of my favorite parts of the day.

—Facebook post, August 26, 2016

GOVERNMENT, DEMOCRACY, AND FREEDOM

In the end, if the people cannot trust their government to do the job for which it exists—to protect them and to promote their common welfare—all else is lost.

> —*"An Honest Government, A Hopeful Future" speech,*
> *University of Nairobi, Kenya, August 28, 2006*

• ◆ •

The patriots of 1776 did not fight to replace the tyranny of a king with the privileges of a few or the rule of a mob. They gave to us a republic, a government of, and by, and for the people, entrusting each generation to keep safe our founding creed. And for more than two hundred years, we have.

> —*Second Inaugural Address, January 21, 2013*

• ◆ •

Moreover, democracy in a nation of more than 300 million people is inherently difficult. It's always been noisy and messy, contentious, complicated. We've been fighting about the proper size and role of government since the day the Framers gathered in Philadelphia. We've battled over the meaning of individual freedom and equality since the Bill of Rights was drafted.

> —*Commencement address, University of Michigan,*
> *Ann Arbor, Michigan, May 1, 2010*

• ◆ •

Progress does not compel us to settle centuries-long debates about the role of government for all time, but it does require us to act in our time.

> —*Second Inaugural Address, January 21, 2013*

• ◆ •

The struggle for the Voting Rights Act taught us that people who love this country can change it. Don't give away your power—go vote.

> —*@POTUS, Twitter, August 6, 2016*

You see, our predecessors understood that government could not, and should not, solve every problem. They understood that there are instances when the gains in security from government action are not worth the added constraints on our freedom. But they also understood that the danger of too much government is matched by the perils of too little; that without the leavening hand of wise policy, markets can crash, monopolies can stifle competition, the vulnerable can be exploited. And they knew that when any government measure, no matter how carefully crafted or beneficial, is subject to scorn; when any efforts to help people in need are attacked as un-American; when facts and reason are thrown overboard and only timidity passes for wisdom, and we can no longer even engage in a civil conversation with each other over the things that truly matter—that at that point we don't merely lose our capacity to solve big challenges. We lose something essential about ourselves.

—*Address to Joint Session of Congress on Health Care, September 9, 2009*

• — •

. . . [D]emocracy isn't a spectator sport. America isn't about "yes he will." It's about "yes we can."

—*Endorsing Hillary Clinton as presidential nominee, Democratic National Convention, Philadelphia, July 27, 2016*

• — •

Democracy works, America, but we got to want it—not just during an election year, but all the days in between.

—*Endorsing Hillary Clinton as presidential nominee, Democratic National Convention, Philadelphia, July 27, 2016*

• — •

Every woman has a constitutional right to make her own reproductive choices. I'm pleased to see the Supreme Court reaffirm that fact today.

—*@POTUS, Twitter, June 27, 2016*

When our government is spoken of as some menacing, threatening foreign entity, it ignores the fact that in our democracy, government is us. We, the people—We, the people, hold in our hands the power to choose our leaders and change our laws, and shape our own destiny.

—Commencement address, University of Michigan, Ann Arbor, Michigan, May 1, 2010

· ◆ ·

Ours, ours is a promise that says government cannot solve all our problems, but what it should do is that which we cannot do for ourselves: protect us from harm and provide every child a decent education; keep our water clean and our toys safe; invest in new schools, and new roads, and new science, and technology.

—Accepting Democratic presidential nomination, Democratic National Convention, Denver, August 28, 2008

· ◆ ·

But democracy does require basic bonds of trust between its citizens. It doesn't work if we think the people who disagree with us are all motivated by malice. It doesn't work if we think that our political opponents are unpatriotic or trying to weaken America. Democracy grinds to a halt without a willingness to compromise, or when even basic facts are contested, or when we listen only to those who agree with us.

—State of the Union Address, Washington, D.C., January 12, 2016

· ◆ ·

If you look at American history, there have been times where we've taken some tough turns, primarily fed by fear and disruptions and dislocations, but with a very substantial exception of the Civil War, generally speaking, the democratic process muddled through and we emerged better and stronger than we were before.

—Interview, National Public Radio, July 1, 2016

You and I, as citizens, have the power to set this country's course. You and I, as citizens, have the obligation to shape the debates of our time—not only with the votes we cast, but with the voices we lift in defense of our most ancient values and enduring ideals.

—Second Inaugural Address, January 21, 2013

· ◆ ·

Our brand of democracy is hard. But I can promise that a little over a year from now, when I no longer hold this office, I will be right there with you as a citizen, inspired by those voices of fairness and vision, of grit and good humor and kindness that helped America travel so far.

—State of the Union Address, Washington, D.C., January 12, 2016

· ◆ ·

We, the people, recognize that we have responsibilities as well as rights; that our destinies are bound together; that a freedom which asks only "What's in it for me," a freedom without a commitment to others, a freedom without love or charity or duty or patriotism, is unworthy of our founding ideals, and those who died in their defense.

—Accepting nomination for second term, Democratic National Convention,
Charlotte, North Carolina, September 6, 2012

· ◆ ·

That's why [f]reedom is not an abstract idea; freedom is the very thing that makes human progress possible—not just at the ballot box, but in our daily lives. One of our greatest Presidents in the United States, Franklin Delano Roosevelt, understood this truth. He defined America's cause as more than the right to cast a ballot. He understood democracy was not just voting. He called upon the world to embrace four fundamental freedoms: freedom of speech, freedom of worship, freedom from want, and freedom from fear. These four freedoms reinforce one another, and you cannot fully realize one without realizing them all.

—Commemorating first United States presidential visit to Burma,
University of Yangon, Rangoon, Burma, November 19, 2012

Our Founders distributed power between states and branches of government, and expected us to argue, just as they did, fiercely, over the size and shape of government, over commerce and foreign relations, over the meaning of liberty and the imperatives of security.

—State of the Union Address, Washington, D.C., January 12, 2016

• ◆ •

These are extraordinary times. The stakes are high and the tensions can sometimes be high as well. But while we'll always have disagreements, I believe that we share the belief that a free press—a press that questions us, that holds us accountable, that sometimes gets under our skin—is absolutely an essential part of our democracy.

—Gridiron Club Dinner, Washington, D.C., March 2013

• ◆ •

Now, I want to be absolutely clear at the start—and I've said this over and over again, this also becomes routine, there is a ritual about this whole thing that I have to do—I believe in the Second Amendment. It's there written on the paper. It guarantees a right to bear arms. No matter how many times people try to twist my words around—I taught constitutional law, I know a little about this—I get it. But I also believe that we can find ways to reduce gun violence consistent with the Second Amendment. I mean, think about it. We all believe in the First Amendment, the guarantee of free speech, but we accept that you can't yell "fire" in a theater. We understand there are some constraints on our freedom in order to protect innocent people. We cherish our right to privacy, but we accept that you have to go through metal detectors before being allowed to board a plane. It's not because people like doing that, but we understand that that's part of the price of living in a civilized society.

—Addressing common-sense gun-safety reform, White House East Room, January 5, 2016

And so if we're serious about freedom of religion—and I'm speaking now to my fellow Christians who remain the majority in this country—we have to understand an attack on one faith is an attack on all our faiths.

—Islamic Society of Baltimore, February 3, 2016

• ◆ •

When we don't vote, we give away our power, disenfranchise ourselves—right when we need to use the power that we have; right when we need your power to stop others from taking away the vote and rights of those more vulnerable than you are—the elderly and the poor, the formerly incarcerated trying to earn their second chance.

—Commencement address, Howard University, Washington, D.C., May 7, 2016

• ◆ •

For history travels not only forwards; history can travel backwards, history can travel sideways. And securing the gains this country has made requires the vigilance of its citizens. Our rights, our freedoms—they are not given. They must be won. They must be nurtured through struggle and discipline, and persistence and faith.

—Lyndon B. Johnson Presidential Library Civil Rights Summit, Austin, Texas, April 10, 2014

• ◆ •

If there's a child on the South Side of Chicago who can't read, that matters to me, even if it's not my child. If there's a senior citizen somewhere who can't pay for their prescription drugs and has to choose between medicine and the rent, that makes my life poorer—even if it's not my grandparent. If there's an Arab-American family being rounded up without benefit of an attorney or due process, that threatens my civil liberties. It is that fundamental belief, it is my fundamental belief—I am my brother's keeper, I am my sister's keeper—that makes this country work.

—Keynote address, Democratic National Convention, Boston, July 27, 2004

EQUALITY AND JUSTICE

We, the people, declare today that the most evident of truths—that all of us are created equal—is the star that guides us still; just as it guided our forebears through Seneca Falls, and Selma, and Stonewall; just as it guided all those men and women, sung and unsung, who left footprints along this great Mall, to hear a preacher say that we cannot walk alone; to hear a King proclaim that our individual freedom is inextricably bound to the freedom of every soul on Earth.

—Second Inaugural Address, January 21, 2013

. ◆ .

We gather here to celebrate them. We gather here to honor the courage of ordinary Americans willing to endure billy clubs and the chastening rod; tear gas and the trampling hoof; men and women who despite the gush of blood and splintered bone would stay true to their North Star and keep marching towards justice.

—Fiftieth anniversary of the Selma-to-Montgomery marches,
Edmund Pettus Bridge, Selma, Alabama, March 7, 2015

. ◆ .

Because of the Civil Rights movement, because of the laws President Johnson signed, new doors of opportunity and education swung open for everybody—not all at once, but they swung open. Not just blacks and whites, but also women and Latinos; and Asians and Native Americans; and gay Americans and Americans with a disability. They swung open for you, and they swung open for me. And that's why I'm standing here today—because of those efforts, because of that legacy.

—Lyndon B. Johnson Presidential Library Civil Rights
Summit, Austin, Texas, April 10, 2014

. ◆ .

. . . [F]or if we are truly created equal, then surely the love we commit to one another must be equal as well.

—Second Inaugural Address, January 21, 2013

Black women were central in the fight for women's rights, from suffrage to the feminist movement—and yet despite their leadership, too often they were also marginalized. But they didn't give up, they didn't let up. They were too fierce for that.

—Congressional Black Caucus, Washington, D.C., September 19, 2015

•-•-•

Because of what they did, the doors of opportunity swung open not just for black folks, but for every American. Their endeavors gave the entire South the chance to rise again, not by reasserting the past, but by transcending the past.

—Fiftieth anniversary of the Selma-to-Montgomery marches, Edmund Pettus Bridge, Selma, Alabama, March 7, 2015

•-•-•

Equality is not just an abstraction, it's not just a formality. It has to go hand in hand with economic opportunity; that in order to address the enduring legacy of slavery and Jim Crow, we've got to make it easier for every American to earn their piece of the American Dream.

—Congressional Black Caucus Foundation Phoenix Awards Dinner, Washington, D.C., September 22, 2013

•-•-•

And this ruling is a victory for America. This decision affirms what millions of Americans already believe in their hearts: When all Americans are treated as equal we are all more free.

—Commending the Supreme Court decision on marriage equality, White House Rose Garden, June 26, 2015

Today is a big step in our march toward equality. Gay and lesbian couples now have the right to marry, just like anyone else. #LoveWins

—@POTUS, Twitter, June 26, 2015

· ◆ ·

What an extraordinary achievement. What a vindication of the belief that ordinary people can do extraordinary things. What a reminder of what Bobby Kennedy once said about how small actions can be like pebbles being thrown into a still lake, and ripples of hope cascade outwards and change the world.

—Commending the Supreme Court decision on marriage equality, White House Rose Garden, June 26, 2015

· ◆ ·

For more than two centuries, we have strived, often at great cost, to form "a more perfect union"—to make sure that "we, the people" applies to all the people. Many of us are only here because others fought to secure rights and opportunities for us. And we've got a responsibility to do the same for future generations.

—Signing of the Executive Order on LGBT Workplace Discrimination, White House East Room, July 21, 2014

· ◆ ·

We shall overcome. We, the citizens of the United States. Like Dr. King, like Abraham Lincoln, like countless citizens who have driven this country inexorably forward, President Johnson knew that ours in the end is a story of optimism, a story of achievement and constant striving that is unique upon this Earth. He knew because he had lived that story. He believed that together we can build an America that is more fair, more equal, and more free than the one we inherited. He believed we make our own destiny. And in part because of him, we must believe it as well.

—Lyndon B. Johnson Presidential Library Civil Rights Summit, Austin, Texas, April 10, 2014

The arc of the moral universe may bend towards justice, but it doesn't bend on its own.

—Fiftieth anniversary of the March on Washington, Lincoln Memorial, Washington, D.C., August 28, 2013

• ◆ •

Today, we are closer to fulfilling America's promise of economic and social justice because we stand on the shoulders of giants like Dr. King, yet our future progress will depend on how we prepare our next generation of leaders. We must fortify their ladders of opportunity by correcting social injustice, breaking the cycle of poverty in struggling communities, and reinvesting in our schools. Education can unlock a child's potential and remains our strongest weapon against injustice and inequality.

—Presidential Proclamation, Martin Luther King Jr. Day, January 15, 2010

• ◆ •

150 years since the abolition of slavery, a turning point in our history. Progress—that's our story.

—@POTUS, Twitter, December 9, 2015

• ◆ •

Today we honor a man who challenged us to bend the arc of the moral universe toward justice. Let's keep working to realize Dr. King's dream.

—@POTUS, Twitter, January 18, 2016

• ◆ •

. . . [F]or all the cruelty and hardship of our world, we are not mere prisoners of fate. Our actions matter, and can bend history in the direction of justice.

—Acceptance speech for the Nobel Peace Prize, Oslo, Norway, December 10, 2009

THE ECONOMY, LABOR,
AND BUSINESS

But this crisis has reminded us that without a watchful eye, the market can spin out of control. The nation cannot prosper long when it favors only the prosperous. The success of our economy has always depended not just on the size of our gross domestic product, but on the reach of our prosperity, on the ability to extend opportunity to every willing heart—not out of charity, but because it is the surest route to our common good.

—Inaugural Address, Washington, D.C., January 21, 2009

Are we going to double down on the top-down economic policies that helped to get us into this mess? Or do we embrace a new economic patriotism that says America does best when the middle class does best?

—Presidential debate, University of Denver, October 3, 2012

So the basic bargain at the heart of our economy has frayed. In fact, this trend towards growing inequality is not unique to America's market economy. Across the developed world, inequality has increased. Some of you may have seen just last week, the Pope himself spoke about this at eloquent length. "How can it be," he wrote, "that it is not a news item when an elderly homeless person dies of exposure, but it is news when the stock market loses two points?" . . . So let me repeat: The combined trends of increased inequality and decreasing mobility pose a fundamental threat to the American Dream, our way of life, and what we stand for around the globe.

—Addressing economic mobility, Town Hall Education Arts Recreation Campus, Washington, D.C., December 4, 2013

There is an important reason that so many working families feel like the system is rigged, and it's because the economy hasn't caught up to some of the enormous changes that have transformed America over the past fifty years. Those days when the average family was a dad who went to work every day and a mom who stayed at home and did all the unpaid labor—that's not what our economy looks like anymore. Household and work arrangements come in all shapes and all combinations, and yet, our workplace policies still look like they're straight out of *Mad Men*.

—*United States of Women Summit, Washington, D.C., June 14, 2016*

. ◆ .

Imagine—these people would slave away in these plants all day long, freezing in the winter and sweltering in the summer, watching coworkers get their bones crushed in machines and friends get fired for even uttering the word "union"—and yet after they punched their card at the end of the day they organized. They went to meetings and they passed out leaflets. They put aside decades of ethnic and racial tension and elected women, African-Americans, and immigrants to leadership positions so that they could speak with one voice.

—*AFL-CIO National Convention, Chicago, July 25, 2005*

. ◆ .

It was the labor movement that helped secure so much of what we take for granted today. The forty-hour work week, the minimum wage, family leave, health insurance, Social Security, Medicare, retirement plans. The cornerstones of the middle-class security all bear the union label.

—*Laborfest, Milwaukee, September 6, 2010*

Let me start with the economy, and a basic fact: The United States of America, right now, has the strongest, most durable economy in the world. We're in the middle of the longest streak of private sector job creation in history. More than 14 million new jobs, the strongest two years of job growth since the '90s, an unemployment rate cut in half. Our auto industry just had its best year ever. That's just part of a manufacturing surge that's created nearly 900,000 new jobs in the past six years. And we've done all this while cutting our deficits by almost three-quarters. Anyone claiming that America's economy is in decline is peddling fiction.

—*State of the Union Address, Washington, D.C., January 12, 2016*

• ◆ •

So my grandparents taught me early on that a job is about more than just a paycheck. A paycheck is important. But a job is about waking up every day with a sense of purpose, and going to bed each night feeling you've handled your responsibilities. It's about meeting your responsibilities to yourself and to your family and to your community.

—*Laborfest, Milwaukee, September 6, 2010*

• ◆ •

Of course Americans build their own businesses. Every day, hardworking people sacrifice to meet a payroll, create jobs, and make our economy run. And what I said was that we need to stand behind them, as America always has, by investing in education and training, roads and bridges, research and technology.

—*Campaign commercial, July 24, 2012*

Entrepreneurship is a fundamental American value. It's also a force for good that unlocks opportunity for people here at home and around the world. But wherever you are, starting your own business isn't easy. It takes access to capital, the right networks, and good mentors. That's why successful entrepreneurs have a unique responsibility to reach back and help those hoping to follow in their footsteps.

—*Facebook post, June 24, 2016*

• ◆ •

We didn't become the most prosperous country in the world just by rewarding greed and recklessness. We didn't come this far by letting the special interests run wild. We didn't do it just by gambling and chasing paper profits on Wall Street. We built this country by making things, by producing goods we could sell.

—*Laborfest, Milwaukee, September 6, 2010*

GUN VIOLENCE AND CRIME

We can't accept events like this as routine. Are we really prepared to say that we're powerless in the face of such carnage, that the politics are too hard? Are we prepared to say that such violence visited on our children year after year after year is somehow the price of our freedom?

—Interfaith prayer vigil after Sandy Hook school shootings, Newtown, Connecticut, December 16, 2012

Citizenship means standing up for the lives that gun violence steals from us each day. I have seen the courage of parents, students, pastors, and police officers all over this country who say, "We are not afraid," and I intend to keep trying, with or without Congress, to help stop more tragedies from visiting innocent Americans in our movie theaters, shopping malls, or schools like Sandy Hook.

—State of the Union Address, Washington, D.C., January 28, 2014

And what's often ignored in this debate is that a majority of gun owners actually agree. A majority of gun owners agree that we can respect the Second Amendment while keeping an irresponsible, law-breaking feud from inflicting harm on a massive scale.

—Addressing common-sense gun-safety reform, White House East Room, January 5, 2016

Gun violence requires more than moments of silence. It requires action. In failing that test, the Senate failed the American people.

—@POTUS, Twitter, June 21, 2016

The gun lobby may be holding Congress hostage, but they can't hold America hostage. We can't accept this carnage in our communities.

—@POTUS, Twitter, January 4, 2016

. ◆ .

Our right to peaceful assembly—that right was robbed from moviegoers in Aurora and Lafayette. Our unalienable right to life, and liberty, and the pursuit of happiness—those rights were stripped from college students in Blacksburg and Santa Barbara, and from high schoolers at Columbine, and from first-graders in Newtown. First-graders.

—Addressing common-sense gun-safety reform, White House East Room, January 5, 2016

. ◆ .

A few months ago, in response to too many tragedies . . . this country took up the cause of protecting more of our people from gun violence. Families that know unspeakable grief summoned the courage to petition their elected leaders—not just to honor the memory of their children, but to protect the lives of all our children. And a few minutes ago, a minority in the United States Senate decided it wasn't worth it. They blocked common-sense gun reforms even while these families looked on from the Senate gallery. . . . So all in all, this was a pretty shameful day for Washington. But this effort is not over. I want to make it clear to the American people we can still bring about meaningful changes that reduce gun violence, so long as the American people don't give up on it.

—Addressing gun violence with Sandy Hook school parent Mark Barden, White House Rose Garden, April 17, 2013

. ◆ .

We cannot accept our level of gun violence as the new normal. We must take action to prevent this from happening again and again.

—@POTUS, Twitter, June 2, 2016

Gun violence requires more than moments of silence. It requires action. In failing that test, the Senate failed the American people.

—*@POTUS, Twitter, June 21, 2016*

• ◆ •

There is no contradiction between us caring about our law enforcement officers and also making sure that our laws are applied fairly. Do not make this as an either/or proposition. This is a both/and proposition. We want to protect our police officers. We'll do a better job doing it if our communities can feel confident that they are being treated fairly.

—*Congressional Black Caucus, Washington, D.C., September 19, 2015*

• ◆ •

Mass incarceration doesn't work. Let's build communities that give kids a shot at success and prisons that prepare people for a 2nd chance.

—*@POTUS, Twitter, July 14, 2015*

• ◆ •

Together, we can raise the level of mutual trust that policing is built on—the idea that police officers are members of the community they risk their lives to protect, and citizens in Ferguson and New York and Cleveland, they just want the same thing young people here marched for fifty years ago—the protection of the law. Together, we can address unfair sentencing and overcrowded prisons, and the stunted circumstances that rob too many boys of the chance to become men, and rob the nation of too many men who could be good dads, and good workers, and good neighbors.

—*Fiftieth anniversary of the Selma-to-Montgomery marches,
Edmund Pettus Bridge, Selma, Alabama, March 7, 2015*

My fellow Americans, only we can prove, through words and through deeds, that we will not be divided. And we're going to have to keep on doing it "again and again and again." That's how this country gets united. That's how we bring people of good will together. Only we can prove that we have the grace and the character and the common humanity to end this kind of senseless violence, to reduce fear and mistrust within the American family, to set an example for our children.

—Statement on the day of Baton Rouge, Louisiana, police officer shootings, White House, July 17, 2016

The United States of America is not the only country on Earth with violent or dangerous people. We are not inherently more prone to violence. But we are the only advanced country on Earth that sees this kind of mass violence erupt with this kind of frequency. It doesn't happen in other advanced countries. It's not even close. And as I've said before, somehow we've become numb to it and we start thinking that this is normal.

—Addressing common-sense gun-safety reform, White House East Room, January 5, 2016

Understand, our police officers put their lives on the line for us every single day. They've got a tough job to do to maintain public safety and hold accountable those who break the law.

—Statement after grand jury decision in Michael Brown/Ferguson, Missouri, shooting case, White House, November 24, 2014

WWW.BARACKOBAMA.COM

CHANGE
WE CAN BELIEVE IN

REFORM AND ACCOMPLISHMENTS

The idea that so many children are born into poverty in the wealthiest nation on Earth is heartbreaking enough. But the idea that a child may never be able to escape that poverty because she lacks a decent education or health care, or a community that views her future as their own, that should offend all of us and it should compel us to action. We are a better country than this.

—Addressing economic mobility, Town Hall Education Arts Recreation Campus, Washington, D.C., December 4, 2013

I understand how difficult this health care debate has been. I know that many in this country are deeply skeptical that government is looking out for them. I understand that the politically safe move would be to kick the can further down the road—to defer reform one more year, or one more election, or one more term. But that's not what the moment calls for. That's not what we came here to do. We did not come to fear the future. We came here to shape it. I still believe we can act even when it's hard. I still believe we can replace acrimony with civility, and gridlock with progress. I still believe we can do great things, and that here and now we will meet history's test.

—Address to Joint Session of Congress on Health Care, Washington, D.C., September 9, 2009

Launching a pilot program to help students in prison pay for college, because everyone willing to work for it deserves a second chance.

—@POTUS, Twitter, July 31, 2015

Five years ago today, I signed a bipartisan bill repealing "Don't Ask, Don't Tell"—extending our country's promise of equality to those who protect it every day. Today, Americans can serve the country they love no matter who they love, and openly gay, lesbian and bisexual men and women in uniform make our military stronger and America safer.

—Facebook post, December 22, 2015

•◆•

Now, let there be no doubt, it will take an unprecedented effort on all our parts—from the halls of Congress to the boardroom, from the union hall to the factory floor—to see the auto industry through these difficult times. And I want every American to know that the path I'm laying out today is our best chance to make sure that the cars of the future are built where they've always been built—in Detroit and across the Midwest—to make America's auto industry in the twenty-first century what it was in the twentieth century—unsurpassed around the world.

—Announcing emergency loans for automotive industry,
White House, March 30, 2009

•◆•

In signing this bill today, I intend to send a clear message: That making our economy work means making sure it works for everyone. That there are no second-class citizens in our workplaces, and that it's not just unfair and illegal—but bad for business—to pay someone less because of their gender, age, race, ethnicity, religion, or disability.

—Statement on signing of Lilly Ledbetter Fair Pay Restoration
Act, Washington, D.C., January 29, 2009

I will repeat what I said 4 years ago when the Supreme Court upheld the ACA: I am as confident as ever that looking back 20 years from now, the nation will be better off because of having the courage to pass this law and persevere. As this progress with health care reform in the United States demonstrates, faith in responsibility, belief in opportunity, and ability to unite around common values are what makes this nation great.

—*Article written for* Journal of the American Medical Association, *August 2, 2016*

We need to give every child, no matter what they look like, where they live, the chance to reach their full potential. Because if we do—if we help these wonderful young men become better husbands and fathers, and well-educated, hardworking, good citizens—then not only will they contribute to the growth and prosperity of this country, but they will pass those lessons on to their children, on to their grandchildren, will start a different cycle. And this country will be richer and stronger for it for generations to come.

—*Announcing "My Brother's Keeper" initiative, February 27, 2014*

• ◆ •

We need equal pay for equal work. We need paid family and sick leave. We need affordable child care. We've got to raise the minimum wage. If we're truly a nation of family values, we wouldn't put up with the fact that many women can't even get a paid day off to give birth. We should guarantee paid maternity leave and paid paternity leave, too. That's how you value families.

—*United States of Women Summit, Washington, D.C., June 14, 2016*

RACE AND RACISM

I am the son of a black man from Kenya and a white woman from Kansas. I was raised with the help of a white grandfather who survived a Depression to serve in Patton's Army during World War II and a white grandmother who worked on a bomber assembly line at Fort Leavenworth while he was overseas. I've gone to some of the best schools in America and lived in one of the world's poorest nations. I am married to a black American who carries within her the blood of slaves and slaveowners—an inheritance we pass on to our two precious daughters. I have brothers, sisters, nieces, nephews, uncles and cousins, of every race and every hue, scattered across three continents, and for as long as I live, I will never forget that in no other country on Earth is my story even possible.

—*"A More Perfect Union" campaign speech, National Constitution Center, Philadelphia, March 18, 2008*

• ◆ •

My view has always been that I'm African-American. African-American by definition, we're a hybrid people. One of the things I loved about my mother was not only did she not feel rejected by me defining myself as an African-American, but she recognized that I was a black man in the United States and my experiences were going to be different than hers.

—*Interview*, Chicago Tribune, *March 15, 2004*

• ◆ •

Our television shows should have some Muslim characters that are unrelated to national security, because, it's not that hard to do. There was a time when there were no black people on television.

—*Islamic Society of Baltimore, February 3, 2016*

There are very few African-American men in this country who haven't had the experience of being followed when they were shopping in a department store. That includes me. There are very few African-American men who haven't had the experience of walking across the street and hearing the locks click on the doors of cars. . . . There are very few African-Americans who haven't had the experience of getting on an elevator and a woman clutching her purse nervously and holding her breath until she had a chance to get off. That happens often.

—Addressing Trayvon Martin ruling, White House, July 19, 2013

• ◆ •

A lack of economic opportunity among black men, and the shame and frustration that came from not being able to provide for one's family, contributed to the erosion of black families—a problem that welfare policies for many years may have worsened. And the lack of basic services in so many urban black neighborhoods—parks for kids to play in, police walking the beat, regular garbage pick-up and building code enforcement—all helped create a cycle of violence, blight and neglect that continue to haunt us.

—"A More Perfect Union" campaign speech, National Constitution Center, Philadelphia, March 18, 2008

• ◆ •

[O]ne of the most durable and destructive legacies of discrimination is the way we've internalized a sense of limitation; how so many in our community have come to expect so little from the world and from themselves.

—NAACP Centennial Convention, New York City, July 16, 2009

There has been talk about should we convene a conversation on race. I haven't seen that be particularly productive when politicians try to organize conversations. . . . On the other hand, in families and churches and workplaces, there's the possibility that people are a little bit more honest, and at least you ask yourself your own questions about, am I wringing as much bias out of myself as I can? Am I judging people as much as I can, based on not the color of their skin, but the content of their character? That would, I think, be an appropriate exercise in the wake of this tragedy.

—Addressing Trayvon Martin ruling, White House, July 19, 2013

• ◆ •

Maybe we now realize the way racial bias can infect us even when we don't realize it, so that we're guarding against not just racial slurs, but we're also guarding against the subtle impulse to call Johnny back for a job interview, but not Jamal. So that we search our hearts when we consider laws to make it harder for some of our fellow citizens to vote.

—Eulogy for Reverend Clementa C. Pinckney,
Charleston, South Carolina, June 26, 2015

• ◆ •

We do a disservice to the cause of justice by intimating that bias and discrimination are immutable, that racial division is inherent to America. If you think nothing's changed in the past fifty years, ask somebody who lived through the Selma or Chicago or Los Angeles of the 1950s.

—Fiftieth anniversary of the Selma-to-Montgomery marches,
Edmund Pettus Bridge, Selma, Alabama, March 7, 2015

• ◆ •

South Carolina taking down the confederate flag—a signal of good will and healing, and a meaningful step towards a better future.

—@POTUS, Twitter, July 10, 2015

I always tell young people in America, "Do not say that nothing's changed when it comes to race in America unless you lived through being a black man in the 1950s or Sixties or Seventies." It is incontrovertible that race relations have improved significantly during my lifetime and yours and that opportunities have opened up and that attitudes have changed. That is a fact. What is also true is that the legacy of slavery, Jim Crow, discrimination in almost every institution of our lives, that casts a long shadow and that's still part of our DNA that's passed on.

—Interview with Marc Maron, WTF podcast, June 19, 2015

• ◆ •

But I have asserted a firm conviction—a conviction rooted in my faith in God and my faith in the American people—that working together we can move beyond some of our old racial wounds, and that in fact we have no choice if we are to continue on the path of a more perfect union.

—"A More Perfect Union" campaign speech, National Constitution
Center, Philadelphia, March 18, 2008

• ◆ •

Yes, African-Americans have felt the cold weight of shackles and the stinging lash of the field whip. But we've also dared to run north, and sing songs from Harriet Tubman's hymnal. We've buttoned up our Union Blues to join the fight for our freedom. We've railed against injustice for decade upon decade—a lifetime of struggle, and progress, and enlightenment that we see etched in Frederick Douglass's mighty, leonine gaze.

—Dedication of the National Museum of African American History
and Culture, Washington, D.C., September 24, 2016

WOMEN

I may be a little grayer than I was eight years ago, but this is what a feminist looks like.

—United States of Women Summit, Washington, D.C., June 14, 2016

• ◆ •

Now, the most important people in my life have always been women. I was raised by a single mom, who spent much of her career working to empower women in developing countries. I watched as my grandmother, who helped raise me, worked her way up at a bank only to hit a glass ceiling. I've seen how Michelle has balanced the demands of a busy career and raising a family. . . . I can look back now and see that, while I helped out, it was usually on my schedule and on my terms. The burden disproportionately and unfairly fell on Michelle.

—Essay, Glamour, *August 4, 2016*

• ◆ •

We can all agree that we've got too many mothers out there forced to do everything all by themselves. They're doing a heroic job, often under trying circumstances. They deserve a lot of credit for that. But they shouldn't have to do it alone. The work of raising our children is the most important job in this country, and it's all of our responsibilities—mothers and fathers.

—Fatherhood Town Hall, White House East Room, June 19, 2009

• ◆ •

Women make up half this country; half its workforce; more than half of our college students. They are not going to succeed the way they should unless they are treated as true equals, and are supported and respected. And unless women are allowed to fulfill their full potential, America will not reach its full potential.

—Introducing "It's On Us" campaign, White House East Room, September 19, 2014

Every little girl I meet out there, I think about Malia and Sasha, and the notion that they'd be treated differently, trapped, not paid enough, having to settle for a raw deal on the job, having to scramble between taking care of kids, taking care of an aging parent, being single moms like my mom was and going to school and work at the same time, then having to come home and cook.

—Interview, Parade, *June 20, 2014*

•◆•

We have to make a collective effort to address violence and abuse against women in all of our communities. In every community, on every campus, we've got to be very clear: Women who have been victims of rape or domestic abuse, who need help, should know that they can count on society and on law enforcement to treat them with love and care and sensitivity, and not skepticism.

—Congressional Black Caucus, Washington, D.C., September 19, 2015

•◆•

Let girls learn so they can help start new ventures and drive economies. Let girls learn so that they can invest in their communities. Let girls learn so they can be safe from violence and abuse. Let girls learn so they can realize their dreams. Because when women have equal futures, families and communities and countries are stronger.

—White House Summit on Global Development, Ronald Reagan Building, Washington, D.C., July 20, 2016

We need to keep changing the attitude that raises our girls to be demure, and our boys to be assertive; that criticizes our daughters for speaking out, and our sons for shedding a tear. We need to change the attitude that punishes women for their sexuality but gives men a pat on the back for theirs. We need to change an Internet where women are routinely harassed and threatened when they go online. We need to keep changing the attitude that congratulates men for changing a diaper, stigmatizes full-time dads, penalizes working moms. We need to keep changing the attitude that prioritizes being confident, competitive, and ambitious in the workplace—unless you're a woman. We need to keep changing a culture that shines a particularly unforgiving light on women and girls of color. About how they look, about how they feel, about what they should or should not do.

—United States of Women Summit, Washington, D.C., June 14, 2016

We must carry forward the work of the women who came before us and ensure our daughters have no limits on their dreams, no obstacle to their achievements, and no remaining ceilings to shatter.

—Presidential Proclamation, Women's History Month, February 28, 2011

When women of color aren't given the opportunity to live up to their God-given potential, we all lose out on their talents; we're not as good a country as we can be. We might miss out on the next Mae Jemison or Ursula Burns or Serena Williams or Michelle Obama.

—Congressional Black Caucus, Washington, D.C., September 19, 2015

Empowering women across the globe is not simply the right thing to do, it is also smart foreign policy.

—Presidential Proclamation, Women's History Month, February 28, 2011

Forty years after the Supreme Court affirmed a woman's constitutional right to privacy, including the right to choose, we shouldn't have to remind people that when it comes to a woman's health, no politician should get to decide what's best for you. No insurer should get to decide what kind of care that you get. The only person who should get to make decisions about your health is you.

—*Planned Parenthood Conference, Washington, D.C., April 26, 2013*

Two hundred and forty years after our nation's founding, and almost a century after women finally won the right to vote, for the first time ever, a woman is a major political party's presidential nominee. No matter your political views, this is a historic moment for America. And it's just one more example of how far women have come on the long journey toward equality.

—*Essay, Glamour, August 4, 2016*

But our country is not just all about the Benjamins—it's about the Tubmans, too. We need all our young people to know that Clara Barton and Lucretia Mott and Sojourner Truth and Eleanor Roosevelt and Dorothy Height, those aren't just for Women's History Month. They're the authors of our history, women who shaped their destiny.

—*United States of Women Summit, Washington, D.C., June 14, 2016*

Today, young women in America grow up knowing an historic truth— that not only can they cast a vote, but they can also run for office and help shape the very democracy that once left them out. For these women, and for generations of women to come, we must keep building a more equal America—whether through the stories we tell about our Nation's history or the faces we display on our country's currency.

—*Presidential Proclamation, Women's Equality Day, August 25, 2016*

THE ENVIRONMENT

We have to all shoulder the responsibility for keeping the planet habitable, or we're going to suffer the consequences—together.

—Addressing climate change, Georgetown University, Washington, D.C., June 25, 2013

・◆・

[T]his is not some distant problem of the future. This is a problem that is affecting Americans right now. Whether it means increased flooding, greater vulnerability to drought, more severe wildfires—all these things are having an impact on Americans as we speak.

—Interview, The Today Show, *May 7, 2014*

・◆・

We don't have time for a meeting of the Flat Earth Society.

—Addressing climate change, Georgetown University, Washington, D.C., June 25, 2013

・◆・

The shift to a cleaner energy economy won't happen overnight, and it will require tough choices along the way. But the debate is settled. Climate change is a fact. And when our children's children look us in the eye and ask if we did all we could to leave them a safer, more stable world, with new sources of energy, I want us to be able to say yes, we did.

—State of the Union Address, Washington, D.C., January 28, 2014

・◆・

Addressing climate change takes all of us, especially the private sector going all-in on clean energy worldwide.

—@POTUS, Twitter, November 30, 2015

Now, part of what's unique about climate change, though, is the nature of some of the opposition to action. It's pretty rare that you'll encounter somebody who says the problem you're trying to solve simply doesn't exist. When President Kennedy set us on a course for the moon, there were a number of people who made a serious case that it wouldn't be worth it; it was going to be too expensive, it was going to be too hard, it would take too long. But nobody ignored the science. I don't remember anybody saying that the moon wasn't there or that it was made of cheese.

—Commencement Address, University of California at Irvine,
Angel Stadium, Anaheim, California, June 14, 2014

• ◆ •

Look, if anybody still wants to dispute the science around climate change, have at it. You will be pretty lonely, because you'll be debating our military, most of America's business leaders, the majority of the American people, almost the entire scientific community, and two hundred nations around the world who agree it's a problem and intend to solve it.

—State of the Union Address, Washington, D.C., January 12, 2016

• ◆ •

[T]hat bright blue ball rising over the moon's surface, containing everything we hold dear—the laughter of children, a quiet sunset, all the hopes and dreams of posterity—that's what's at stake. That's what we're fighting for. And if we remember that, I'm absolutely sure we'll succeed.

—Addressing climate change, Georgetown University,
Washington, D.C., June 25, 2013

Today, the U.S. joined some 170 nations to sign the Paris Agreement—an historic step this Earth Day to protect the one planet we've got.

—@POTUS, Twitter, April 22, 2016

There's still much more to do. But there's no doubt that America has become a global leader in the fight against climate change. Last year, that leadership helped us bring nearly 200 nations together in Paris around the most ambitious agreement in history to save the one planet we've got. That's not something to tear up—it's something to build upon. And if we keep pushing, and leading the world in the right direction, there's no doubt that, together, we can leave a better, cleaner, safer future for our children.

—Weekly address, White House, August 13, 2016

As President, I'm proud to have built upon America's tradition of conservation. We've protected more than 265 million acres of public lands and waters—more than any administration in history. We've recovered endangered wildlife species and restored vulnerable ecosystems. We've designated new monuments to Cesar Chavez in California, the Pullman porters in Chicago, and the folks who stood up for equality at Stonewall in New York—to better reflect the full history of our nation. And we've got more work to do to preserve our lands, culture, and history. So we're not done yet.

—Weekly address, White House, August 20, 2016

[Climate change] is a political problem perfectly designed to repel government intervention. It involves every single country, and it is a comparatively slow-moving emergency, so there is always something seemingly more urgent on the agenda.

—*Interview,* The Atlantic*, April 2016*

This "blue marble" belongs to all of us. It belongs to these kids who are here. There are more than 7 billion people alive today; no matter what country they're from, no matter what language they speak, every one of them can look at this image and say, "That's my home." And "we're the first generation to feel the impact of climate change; we're the last generation that can do something about it." We only get one home. We only get one planet. There's no plan B.

—*Announcing Clean Power Plan, White House East Room, August 3, 2015*

KNOWLEDGE, EDUCATION,
AND INNOVATION

At the dawn of the twenty-first century, where knowledge is literally power, where it unlocks the gates of opportunity and success, we all have responsibilities as parents, as librarians, as educators, as politicians, and as citizens to instill in our children a love of reading so that we can give them a chance to fulfill their dreams. That's what all of you do each and every day, and for that, I am grateful.

—*American Library Association Annual Conference, Chicago, 2005*

. ◆ .

Education was the gateway to opportunity for me. It was the gateway for Michelle. It was the gateway for most of you. And now more than ever it is the gateway to a middle-class life.

—*Democratic National Convention, Charlotte, North Carolina, September 6, 2012*

. ◆ .

To my 5th grade teacher Ms. Mabel Hefty and the educators who inspire our young people every single day: Thank you.

—*@POTUS, Twitter, May 3, 2016*

. ◆ .

And government has a role in this. But teachers must inspire; principals must lead; parents must instill a thirst for learning. And, students, you've got to do the work. And together, I promise you, we can out-educate and out-compete any nation on Earth.

—*Democratic National Convention, Charlotte, North Carolina, September 6, 2012*

So all of you budding entrepreneurs, don't be shy while you're here. Talk to the experts here. Make your pitch. Network with potential investors. Find that mentor who might help you navigate through a tough patch. Connect with your fellow innovators. Because ultimately the world needs your creativity, and your energy, and your vision. You are going to be what helps this process of global integration work in a way that is good for everyone and not just some.

—Global Entrepreneurship Summit,
Stanford University, California, July 25, 2016

• ◆ •

Cool clock, Ahmed. Want to bring it to the White House? We should inspire more kids like you to like science. It's what makes America great.

—To Muslim boy who'd been arrested after teachers mistook his homemade
clock for a bomb, @POTUS, Twitter, September 15, 2015

• ◆ •

We need scientists to design new fuels. We need farmers to help grow them. We need engineers to invent new technologies. We need entrepreneurs to sell those technologies. We need workers to operate assembly lines that hum with high-tech, zero-carbon components. We need builders to hammer into place the foundations for a clean energy age. We need diplomats and businessmen and women, and Peace Corps volunteers to help developing nations skip past the dirty phase of development and transition to sustainable sources of energy. In other words, we need you.

—Commencement address, University of California at Irvine,
Angel Stadium, Anaheim, California, June 14, 2014

Fortunately, your generation has everything it takes to lead this country toward a brighter future. I'm confident that you can make the right choices—away from fear and division and paralysis, and toward cooperation and innovation and hope.

—*Commencement address, Rutgers University, New Brunswick, New Jersey, May 15, 2016*

In politics and in life, ignorance is not a virtue. It's not cool to not know what you're talking about. That's not keeping it real, or telling it like it is. That's not challenging political correctness. That's just not knowing what you're talking about.

—*Commencement address, Rutgers University, New Brunswick, New Jersey, May 15, 2016*

When Americans are called on to innovate, that's what we do— whether it's making more fuel-efficient cars or more fuel-efficient appliances, or making sure that we are putting in place the kinds of equipment that prevent harm to the ozone layer and eliminate acid rain. At every one of these steps, there have been folks who have said it can't be done. There have been naysayers who said this is going to destroy jobs and destroy industry. And it doesn't happen, because once we have a clear target to meet, we typically meet it. And we find the best ways to do it.

—*Conference call with public health groups, June 2, 2014*

PEACE, WAR, AND
FOREIGN POLICY

Enduring security and lasting peace do not require perpetual war.

—Second Inaugural Address, January 21, 2013

• ◆ •

I do not bring with me today a definitive solution to the problems of war. What I do know is that meeting these challenges will require the same vision, hard work and persistence of those men and women who acted so boldly decades ago. And it will require us to think in new ways about the notions of just war and the imperatives of a just peace.

—Acceptance speech for the Nobel Peace Prize,
Oslo, Norway, December 10, 2009

• ◆ •

When we send our young men and women into harm's way, we have a solemn obligation not to fudge the numbers or shade the truth about why they are going, to care for their families while they're gone, to tend to the soldiers upon their return and to never, ever go to war without enough troops to win the war, secure the peace, and earn the respect of the world.

—Keynote address, Democratic National Convention,
Boston, July 27, 2004

• ◆ •

The brave Americans who fight today believe deeply in this country. And no matter how many you meet, or how many stories of heroism you hear, every encounter reminds that they are truly special. That through their service, they are living out the ideals that stir so many of us as Americans—pride, duty, and sacrifice.

—Campaign speech, Fargo, North Dakota, July 3, 2008

America's commitment to global security will never waver. But in a world in which threats are more diffuse, and missions more complex, America cannot act alone. America alone cannot secure the peace. This is true in Afghanistan. This is true in failed states like Somalia, where terrorism and piracy is joined by famine and human suffering. And sadly, it will continue to be true in unstable regions for years to come.

—*Acceptance speech for the Nobel Peace Prize,*
Oslo, Norway, December 10, 2009

• ◆ •

My grandfather signed up for a war the day after Pearl Harbor was bombed, fought in Patton's army. He saw the dead and dying across the fields of Europe; he heard the stories of fellow troops who first entered Auschwitz and Treblinka. He fought in the name of a larger freedom, part of that arsenal of democracy that triumphed over evil, and he did not fight in vain. I don't oppose all wars. . . . What I am opposed to is a dumb war. What I am opposed to is a rash war.

—*Speaking at anti–Iraq War rally with Jesse Jackson and other politicians*
on the day President George W. Bush signed authorization of force,
Federal Plaza, Chicago, October 2, 2002

• ◆ •

Moreover, we refuse to let terrorists and voices of division undermine the unity and the values of diversity and pluralism that keep our nation strong. One of the reasons that America's armed forces are the best in the world is because we draw on the skills and the talents of all of our citizens, from all backgrounds and faiths, including patriotic Muslim Americans who risk and give their lives for our freedom.

—*Press conference, Pentagon, Washington, D.C., August 4, 2016*

Tonight, I can report to the American people and to the world that the United States has conducted an operation that killed Osama bin Laden, the leader of al Qaeda, and a terrorist who's responsible for the murder of thousands of innocent men, women, and children. It was nearly ten years ago that a bright September day was darkened by the worst attack on the American people in our history. . . . After nearly ten years of service, struggle and sacrifice, we know well the costs of war. These efforts weigh on me every time I, as Commander-in-Chief, have to sign a letter to a family that has lost a loved one, or look into the eyes of a service member who's been gravely wounded. So Americans understand the costs of war. Yet as a country, we will never tolerate our security being threatened, nor stand idly by when our people have been killed. We will be relentless in defense of our citizens and our friends and allies. We will be true to the values that make us who we are. And on nights like this one, we can say to those families who have lost loved ones to al Qaeda's terror: Justice has been done.

—Announcing the death of Osama bin Laden,
White House East Room, May 2, 2011

Protecting the American people is my top priority. With our 65 global partners, we're leading the campaign to degrade and destroy ISIL.

—@POTUS, Twitter, November 18, 2015

[T]he burdens of global citizenship continue to bind us together. . . . Partnership among nations is not a choice; it is the one way, the only way, to protect our common security and advance our common humanity.

—Campaign speech, Berlin, July 24, 2008

If you doubt America's commitment—or mine—to see that justice is done, just ask Osama bin Laden. Ask the leader of al Qaeda in Yemen, who was taken out last year, or the perpetrator of the Benghazi attacks, who sits in a prison cell. When you come after Americans, we go after you. And it may take time, but we have long memories, and our reach has no limits.

—*State of the Union Address, Washington, D.C., January 12, 2016*

• ◆ •

. . . ISIL can't defeat the United States of America or our NATO partners. We can defeat ourselves, though, if we make bad decisions . . . if we start making bad decisions—indiscriminately killing civilians, for example, in some of these areas, instituting offensive religious tests on who can enter the country—those kinds of strategies can end up backfiring. Because in order for us to ultimately win this fight, we cannot frame this as a clash of civilizations between the West and Islam. That plays exactly into the hands of ISIL and the perversions—the perverse interpretations of Islam that they're putting forward.

—*Press conference, Pentagon, Washington, D.C., August 4, 2016*

• ◆ •

The United States of America is the most powerful nation on Earth. Period. Period. It's not even close. . . . We spend more on our military than the next eight nations combined. Our troops are the finest fighting force in the history of the world. No nation attacks us directly, or our allies, because they know that's the path to ruin.

—*State of the Union Address, Washington, D.C., January 12, 2016*

It is not simply their bravery, their insistence on doing their part—whatever the cost—to make America more secure and our world more free. It's not simply an unflinching belief in our highest ideals. It's that in the thick of battle, when their very survival is threatened, America's sons and daughters aren't thinking about themselves, they're thinking about one another; they're risking everything to save not their own lives, but the lives of their fellow soldiers and sailors, airmen and Marines. And when we lose them—in a final act of selflessness and service—we know that they died so that their brothers and sisters, so that our nation, might live.

—*Campaign speech on Memorial Day, Las Cruces, New Mexico, May 26, 2008*

• ◆ •

You see, in a world of complex threats, our security and leadership depends on all elements of our power—including strong and principled diplomacy.

—*State of the Union Address, Washington, D.C., January 28, 2014*

• ◆ •

Dropping bombs on someone to prove that you're willing to drop bombs on someone is just about the worst reason to use force.

—*Interview,* The Atlantic, *April 2016*

• ◆ •

And for America, the choice is clear: We choose hope over fear. We see the future not as something out of our control, but as something we can shape for the better through concerted and collective effort. We reject fatalism or cynicism when it comes to human affairs. We choose to work for the world as it should be, as our children deserve it to be.

—*Address to the United Nations General Assembly,*
New York City, September 24, 2014

We live in a complicated world—a world in which the forces unleashed by human innovation are creating opportunities for our children that were unimaginable for most of human history. It is also a world of persistent threats, a world in which mass violence and cruelty is all too common, and human innovation risks the destruction of all that we hold dear. In this world, the United States of America remains the most powerful nation on Earth, and I believe that we will remain such for decades to come. But we are one nation among many.

—Discussing agreement on Iran nuclear deal, American University, Washington, D.C., August 5, 2015

In Cuba, we are ending a policy that was long past its expiration date. When what you're doing doesn't work for fifty years, it's time to try something new

—State of the Union Address, Washington, D.C., January 20, 2015

I have come here to bury the last remnant of the Cold War in the Americas. I have come here to extend the hand of friendship to the Cuban people.

—Speaking during visit to Cuba after establishing new era of cooperation, Gran Teatro de la Habana, Havana, March 22, 2016

Resist the conventional wisdom and the drumbeat of war. Worry less about being labeled weak; worry more about getting it right.

—Discussing agreement on Iran nuclear deal, American University, Washington, D.C., August 5, 2015

People tell me around the world when I travel, developing nations, they do not just want aid, they want trade. They want capacity-building. As we've seen from South Korea to Chile to Botswana, the developing nation of today can end up being the engine of global growth tomorrow.

—*White House Summit on Global Development, Ronald Reagan Building, Washington, D.C., July 20, 2016*

. ➤ .

Slamming the door in the face of refugees would betray our deepest values. That's not who we are. And it's not what we're going to do.

—*Regarding the Syrian refugee crisis, @POTUS, Twitter, November 18, 2015*

. ➤ .

As someone who begins every day with an intelligence briefing, I know this is a dangerous time. But that's not primarily because of some looming superpower out there, and certainly not because of diminished American strength. In today's world, we're threatened less by evil empires and more by failing states.

—*State of the Union Address, Washington, D.C., January 12, 2016*

. ➤ .

We also can't try to take over and rebuild every country that falls into crisis, even if it's done with the best of intentions. That's not leadership; that's a recipe for quagmire, spilling American blood and treasure that ultimately will weaken us. It's the lesson of Vietnam; it's the lesson of Iraq—and we should have learned it by now.

—*State of the Union Address, Washington, D.C., January 12, 2016*

For all of our warts, the United States has clearly been a force for good in the world. If you compare us to previous superpowers, we act less on the basis of naked self-interest, and have been interested in establishing norms that benefit everyone. If it is possible to do good at a bearable cost, to save lives, we will do it.

—*Interview,* The Atlantic, *April 2016*

．◆．

We must change our mindset about war itself—to prevent conflict through diplomacy, and strive to end conflicts after they've begun; to see our growing interdependence as a cause for peaceful cooperation and not violent competition; to define our nations not by our capacity to destroy, but by what we build. And perhaps above all, we must reimagine our connection to one another as members of one human race.

—*Speaking at Hiroshima Peace Memorial with
Prime Minister Shinzo Abe, May 27, 2016*

．◆．

Each of us as leaders, each nation can choose to reject those who appeal to our worst impulses and embrace those who appeal to our best. For we have shown that we can choose a better history.

—*Address to the 71st Session of the United Nations General Assembly,
New York City, September 20, 2016*

HARDSHIP, HOPE,
AND CHANGE

For all of us, life presents challenges and suffering—accidents, illnesses, the loss of loved ones. There are times when we are overwhelmed by sudden calamity, natural or manmade. All of us, we make mistakes. And at times we are lost. And as we get older, we learn we don't always have control of things—not even a President does. But we do have control over how we respond to the world. We do have control over how we treat one another.

—Memorial service for ambushed, slain Dallas police officers, Dallas, July 12, 2016

I'm only here because this country educated my grandfather on the GI Bill. When my father left and my mom hit hard times trying to raise my sister and me while she was going to school, this country helped make sure we didn't go hungry. When Michelle, the daughter of a shift worker at a water plant and a secretary, wanted to go to college, just like me, this country helped us afford it until we could pay it back.

—Addressing economic mobility, Town Hall Education Arts Recreation Campus, Washington, D.C., December 4, 2013

Hope in the face of difficulty, hope in the face of uncertainty, the audacity of hope: In the end, that is God's greatest gift to us, the bedrock of this nation, a belief in things not seen, a belief that there are better days ahead.

—Keynote address, Democratic National Convention, Boston, July 27, 2004

America is a land of big dreamers and big hopes. It is this hope that has sustained us through revolution and civil war, depression and world war, a struggle for civil and social rights and the brink of nuclear crisis. And it is because of our dreamers that we have emerged from each challenge more united, more prosperous, and more admired than ever before.

—*Commencement address, Knox College, Galesburg, Illinois, June 4, 2005*

But in the unlikely story that is America, there has never been anything false about hope. For when we have faced down impossible odds, when we've been told that we're not ready or that we shouldn't try or that we can't, generations of Americans have responded with a simple creed that sums up the spirit of a people: Yes, we can.

—*Campaign speech to supporters after New Hampshire primary, January 8, 2008*

One voice can change a room. And if the voice can change a room, it can change a city. And if it can change a city, it can change a state. And if it change a state, it can change a nation. And if it can change a nation, it can change the world. . . . [Y]our voice can change the world tomorrow.

—*Campaign speech before election night, Manassas, Virginia, November 3, 2008*

Change will not come if we wait for some other person, or if we wait for some other time. We are the ones we've been waiting for. We are the change that we seek.

—*Chicago, February 5, 2008*

We live in a time of extraordinary change—change that's reshaping the way we live, the way we work, our planet, our place in the world. It's change that promises amazing medical breakthroughs, but also economic disruptions that strain working families. It promises education for girls in the most remote villages, but also connects terrorists plotting an ocean away. It's change that can broaden opportunity, or widen inequality. And whether we like it or not, the pace of this change will only accelerate.

—*State of the Union Address, Washington, D.C.,*
January 12, 2016

Because the world, for all of its travails, for all of its challenges, has never been healthier, better educated, wealthier, more tolerant, less violent, more attentive to the rights of all people than it is today.

—*Town Hall with Young Leaders of the UK, London, April 23, 2016*

Change isn't something that happens every four years or eight years; change is not placing your faith in any particular politician and then just putting your feet up and saying, okay, go. Change is the effort of committed citizens who hitch their wagons to something bigger than themselves and fight for it every single day.

—*Commencement address, Howard University,*
Washington, D.C., May 7, 2016

RELIGION, MORALITY,
AND VALUES

I am a Christian, and I am a devout Christian. I believe in the redemptive death and resurrection of Jesus Christ. I believe that that faith gives me a path to be cleansed of sin and have eternal life. But most importantly, I believe in the example that Jesus set by feeding the hungry and healing the sick and always prioritizing the least of these over the powerful. . . . [T]here was a very strong awakening in me of the importance of these issues in my life. I didn't want to walk alone on this journey. Accepting Jesus Christ in my life has been a powerful guide for my conduct and my values and my ideals.

—*Interview,* Christianity Today, *January 23, 2008*

• ✦ •

I was not raised in a particularly religious household. I had a father who was born a Muslim but became an atheist, grandparents who were non-practicing Methodists and Baptists, and a mother who was skeptical of organized religion, even as she was the kindest, most spiritual person I've ever known. She was the one who taught me as a child to love, and to understand, and to do unto others as I would want done. I didn't become a Christian until many years later, when I moved to the South Side of Chicago after college. It happened not because of indoctrination or a sudden revelation, but because I spent month after month working with church folks who simply wanted to help neighbors who were down on their luck—no matter what they looked like, or where they came from, or who they prayed to. It was on those streets, in those neighborhoods, that I first heard God's spirit beckon me. It was there that I felt called to a higher purpose—His purpose.

—*National Prayer Breakfast, Washington, D.C., February 5, 2009*

Treating others as you want to be treated. Requiring much from those who have been given so much. Living by the principle that we are our brother's keeper. Caring for the poor and those in need. These values are old. They can be found in many denominations and many faiths, among many believers and among many non-believers. And they are values that have always made this country great—when we live up to them; when we don't just give lip service to them; when we don't just talk about them one day a year. And they're the ones that have defined my own faith journey.

—*National Prayer Breakfast, Washington, D.C., February, 2, 2012*

And I will do everything that I can as long as I am President of the United States to remind the American people that we are one nation under God, and we may call that God different names but we remain one nation. And as somebody who relies heavily on my Christian faith in my job, I understand the passions that religious faith can raise. But I'm also respectful that people of different faiths can practice their religion, even if they don't subscribe to the exact same notions that I do, and that they are still good people, and they are my neighbors and they are my friends, and they are fighting alongside us in our battles.

—*Responding to question on suspicion and resentment of Islam, press conference, White House, September 10, 2010*

And so, yes, like every person, there are times where I'm fearful. But my faith and, more importantly, the faith that I've seen in so many of you, the God I see in you, that makes me inevitably hopeful about our future. I have seen so many who know that God has not given us a spirit of fear. He has given us power, and love, and a sound mind.

—*National Prayer Breakfast, Washington, D.C., February 4, 2016*

When we abandon the field of religious discourse—when we ignore the debate about what it means to be a good Christian or Muslim or Jew; when we discuss religion only in the negative sense of where or how it should not be practiced, rather than in the positive sense of what it tells us about our obligations toward one another; when we shy away from religious venues and religious broadcasts because we assume that we will be unwelcome—others will fill the vacuum. And those who do are likely to be those with the most insular views of faith, or who cynically use religion to justify partisan ends.

—The Audacity of Hope

Groups like al Qaeda and ISIL promote a twisted interpretation of religion that is rejected by the overwhelming majority of the world's Muslims. The world must continue to lift up the voices of Muslim clerics and scholars who teach the true peaceful nature of Islam. We can echo the testimonies of former extremists who know how terrorists betray Islam. . . . We know from experience that the best way to protect people, especially young people, from falling into the grip of violent extremists is the support of their family, friends, teachers and faith leaders.

—*Op-ed,* Los Angeles Times, *February 17, 2015*

In fact, because I do not believe that religious people have a monopoly on morality, I would rather have someone who is grounded in morality and ethics, and who is also secular, affirm their morality and ethics and values without pretending that they're something they're not. They don't need to do that. None of us need to do that.

—*Keynote address, "A Call to Renewal," Building a Covenant for a New America conference, Washington, D.C., June 28, 2006*

We need to reject any politics—any politics—that targets people because of race or religion. . . . This is not a matter of political correctness. This is a matter of understanding just what it is that makes us strong. The world respects us not just for our arsenal; it respects us for our diversity, and our openness, and the way we respect every faith. His Holiness, Pope Francis, told this body from the very spot that I'm standing on tonight that "to imitate the hatred and violence of tyrants and murderers is the best way to take their place." When politicians insult Muslims, whether abroad or our fellow citizens, when a mosque is vandalized, or a kid is called names, that doesn't make us safer. That's not telling it like it is. It's just wrong. It diminishes us in the eyes of the world. It makes it harder to achieve our goals. It betrays who we are as a country.

—*State of the Union Address, Washington, D.C., January 12, 2016*

FAMILY

Of all the rocks upon which we build our lives, we are reminded today that family is the most important.

—*Father's Day speech, Apostolic Church of God,*
Chicago, June 25, 2008

It was women, then, who provided the ballast in my life—my grandmother, whose dogged practicality kept the family afloat, and my mother, whose love and clarity of spirit kept my sister's and my world centered. Because of them I never wanted for anything important. From them I would absorb the values that guide me to this day.

—The Audacity of Hope

She helped me understand that America is great not because it is perfect but because it can always be made better—and that the unfinished work of perfecting our union falls to each of us. It's a charge we pass on to our children, coming closer with each new generation to what we know America should be.

—*Writing about his mother, "A Letter to My Daughters,"*
Parade, *August 4, 2013*

In my own family, I have a father who was from Kenya; I have a mother who was from Kansas, in the Midwest of the United States; my sister is half-Indonesian; she's married to a Chinese person from Canada. So when you see family gatherings in the Obama household, it looks like the United Nations.

—*Town Hall with Chinese youth, Shanghai, November 16, 2009*

Fathers are our first teachers and coaches. They're our mentors and they're our role models. They set an example of success and they push us to succeed; encourage us when we're struggling; and they love us even when we disappoint them, and they stand by us when nobody else will.

—Interview about fathers, CBS News, June 21, 2009

• ✦ •

When we work hard, treat others with respect, spend within our means, and contribute to our communities, those are the lessons our children learn. And that is what so many fathers are doing every day—coaching soccer and Little League, going to those school assemblies and parent-teacher conferences, scrimping and saving and working that extra shift so their kids can go to college. They are fulfilling their most fundamental duty as fathers: to show their children, by example, the kind of people they want them to become.

—"We Need Fathers to Step Up," Parade, June 16, 2011

• ✦ •

Every man is trying to live up to his father's expectations or make up for his mistakes. In my case, both things might be true.

—Obama: From Promise to Power, by David Mendell

• ✦ •

I learned that my grandfather had been a cook for the British and, although he was a respected elder in his village, he was called "boy" by his employers for most of his life.

—"An Honest Government, A Hopeful Future" speech,
University of Nairobi, Kenya, August 28, 2006

I learned how my father had grown up on a tiny village called Alego . . . I began to understand and appreciate the distance he had traveled—from being a boy herding goats to a student at the University of Hawaii and Harvard University to the respected economist that he was upon his return to Kenya. In many ways, he embodied the new Africa of the early sixties, a man who had obtained the knowledge of the Western world and sought to bring it back home, where he hoped he could help create a new nation.

—*"An Honest Government, A Hopeful Future" speech,*
University of Nairobi, Kenya, August 28, 2006

Most people who meet my wife quickly conclude that she is remarkable. They are right about this—she is smart, funny, and thoroughly charming. She is also very beautiful. . . . Often, after hearing her speak at some function or working with her on a project, people will approach me and say something to the effect of, "You know I think the world of you, Barack, but your wife . . . wow!" I nod, knowing that if I ever had to run against her for public office, she would beat me without much difficulty.

—The Audacity of Hope

Nurturing families come in many forms, and children may be raised by a father and mother, a single father, two fathers, a step father, a grandfather, or caring guardian. . . . For the character they build, the doors they open, and the love they provide over our lifetimes, all our fathers deserve our unending appreciation and admiration.

—*Presidential Proclamation, Father's Day, June 18, 2010*

Sometimes, when we're lying together, I look at her and I feel dizzy with the realization that here is another distinct person from me, who has memories, origins, thoughts, feelings that are different from my own. That tension between familiarity and mystery meshes something strong between us. Even if one builds a life together based on trust, attentiveness and mutual support, I think that it's important that a partner continues to surprise.

—*Le Monde, 1996*

. ◆ .

When I was a young man, I thought life was all about me—about how I'd make my way in the world, become successful, and get the things I want. But then the two of you came into my world with all your curiosity and mischief and those smiles that never fail to fill my heart and light up my day. And suddenly, all my big plans for myself didn't seem so important anymore. I soon found that the greatest joy in my life was the joy I saw in yours. And I realized that my own life wouldn't count for much unless I was able to ensure that you had every opportunity for happiness and fulfillment in yours. In the end, girls, that's why I ran for President: because of what I want for you and for every child in this nation.

—*"A Letter to My Daughters,"* Parade, *January 18, 2009*

. ◆ .

They're smart and funny, but most importantly they're kind. They don't have attitude.

—*Commenting on his daughters,* The Tonight Show with Jimmy Fallon, *June 9, 2016*

Let's be clear: Just because your own father wasn't there for you, that's not an excuse for you to be absent also—it's all the more reason for you to be present. There's no rule that says that you have to repeat your father's mistakes. Just the opposite—you have an obligation to break the cycle and to learn from those mistakes, and to rise up where your own fathers fell short and to do better than they did with your own children.

—Fatherhood Town Hall, White House East Room, June 19, 2009

. ◆ .

Those family meals, afternoons in the park, bedtime stories; the encouragement we give, the questions we answer, the limits we set, the example we set of persistence in the face of difficulty and hardship—those things add up over time, and they shape a child's character, build their core, teach them to trust in life and to enter into it with confidence and with hope and with determination.

—Introducing Fatherhood and Mentoring Initiative, Town Hall Education Arts Recreation Campus, Washington, D.C., June 21, 2010

. ◆ .

There's only one thing we can be sure of, and that is the love that we have—for our children, for our families, for each other. The warmth of a small child's embrace—that is true. The memories we have of them, the joy that they bring, the wonder we see through their eyes, that fierce and boundless love we feel for them, a love that takes us out of ourselves, and binds us to something larger—we know that's what matters.

—Interfaith prayer vigil after Sandy Hook school shootings, Newtown, Connecticut, December 16, 2012

Over the course of my life, I have been an attorney, I've been a professor, I've been a state senator, I've been a U.S. senator—and I currently am serving as President of the United States. But I can say without hesitation that the most challenging, most fulfilling, most important job I will have during my time on this Earth is to be Sasha and Malia's dad.

—*Introducing Fatherhood and Mentoring Initiative, Town Hall Education Arts Recreation Campus, Washington, D.C., June 21, 2010*

LIFE'S PLEASURES

Now, my best week, I will tell you, was marrying Michelle. That was a really good week. Malia and Sasha being born, excellent weeks. There was a game where I scored 27 points, that was a pretty good week. I've had some good weeks in my life, I will tell you.

—Press conference with Brazilian President Dilma Rousseff, June 30, 2015

•◆•

One of the wrestling matches I'm always having with my staff is getting my kids' events onto the schedule. I have to make sure they understand that's a priority.

—O, the Oprah Magazine, November 2004

•◆•

A few months ago, Michelle, Malia, Sasha, and I traveled to Yosemite National Park. Yosemite is one of America's oldest parks— an iconic cornerstone of our National Park System. It is, without a doubt, one of the most stunning places I've ever been. Standing among the sprawling meadows or beneath the Cathedral Rocks, it's hard not to be awestruck by the unique, natural beauty of our country.

—Facebook post, August 25, 2016

•◆•

I was never great, but I was a good player, and I could play seriously. Now I'm like one of these old guys who's running around, and the guys I play with, who are all a lot younger, they sort of pity me and sympathize with me. They tolerate me, but we all know that I'm the weak link on the court. And I don't like being the weak link.

—Interview with Marc Maron, WTF podcast, June 19, 2015

And for all those who think I golf too much, let me be clear. I'm not spending time on the golf course—I'm investing time on the golf course.

—Gridiron Club Dinner, Washington, D.C., March 12, 2011

⋅◆⋅

It's the only excuse I have to get outside for four hours at a stretch.

—Interview with Hearst magazine editors, quoted widely, April 2011

⋅◆⋅

If you swiped through my music collection, you'd find some Bruce, some Stevie, some Al Green. If you opened my iPad, you'd find the word puzzle games I love to play. If you looked at my bookshelf, you'd find Marilynne Robinson novels and Toni Morrison classics.

—Facebook post, April 28, 2016

⋅◆⋅

I miss being anonymous. I miss Saturday morning, rolling out of bed, not shaving, getting into my car with my girls, driving to the supermarket, squeezing the fruit, getting my car washed, taking walks.

—Interview with Hearst magazine editors, quoted widely, April 2011

⋅◆⋅

It's all happened. I've been through this, I've screwed up, I've been in the barrel tumbling down Niagara Falls, and I emerged, and I lived. And that's such a liberating feeling. It's one of the benefits of age. It almost compensates for the fact I can't play basketball anymore.

—Interview with Marc Maron, WTF podcast, June 19, 2015

PRESIDENTIAL WIT

One of the things I think I can bring to the presidency is to make government and public service cool again.

—*Interview,* Time, *2007*

• ✦ •

Everyone please take your seats, or else Clint Eastwood will yell at them.

—*Alfred E. Smith Memorial Foundation Dinner, Waldorf Towers,*
New York City, October 18, 2012

• ✦ •

In my first term, we ended the war in Iraq; in my second term, I will win the war on Christmas. In my first term, we repealed the policy known as "Don't Ask, Don't Tell"—wait, though; in my second term, we will replace it with a policy known as, "It's raining men." In my first term, we passed health care reform; in my second term, I guess I'll pass it again.

—*White House Correspondents' Dinner,*
Washington, D.C., April 29, 2012

• ✦ •

Governor Romney, I'm glad that you recognize that al Qaeda is a threat because a few months ago when you were asked what's the biggest geopolitical threat facing America, you said Russia, not al Qaeda; you said Russia. The 1980s are now calling and asking for their foreign policy back, because, you know, the Cold War's been over for twenty years.

—*Final 2012 presidential debate with Mitt Romney, Lynn University,*
Boca Raton, Florida, October 22, 2012

I want to especially thank all the members who took a break from their exhausting schedule of not passing any laws to be here tonight.

—*White House Correspondents' Dinner,*
Washington, D.C., April 29, 2012

. ◆ .

I know Republicans are still sorting out what happened in 2012, but one thing they all agree on is they need to do a better job reaching out to minorities. And look, call me self-centered, but I can think of one minority they could start with. Hello? Think of me as a trial run, you know? See how it goes.

—*White House Correspondents' Dinner,*
Washington, D.C., April 27, 2013

. ◆ .

As I was saying, we face major challenges. March in particular is going to be full of tough decisions. But I want to assure you, I have my top advisors working around the clock . . . there is an entire team in the Situation Room as we speak, planning my next golf outing, right now at this moment.

—*Gridiron Club Dinner, Washington, D.C., March 9, 2013*

. ◆ .

[S]ome folks still don't think I spend enough time with Congress. "Why don't you get a drink with Mitch McConnell?" they ask. Really? Why don't you go get a drink with Mitch McConnell?

—*White House Correspondents' Dinner,*
Washington, D.C., April 27, 2013

I've got to stay focused on my job, because for many Americans, this is still a time of deep uncertainty. For example, I have one friend—just a few weeks ago, she was making millions of dollars a year and she's now living out of a van in Iowa.

—*White House Correspondents' Dinner, Washington, D.C., April 25, 2015*

• ◆ •

I tease Joe sometimes, but he has been at my side for seven years. I love that man. He's not just a great vice president, he is a great friend. We've gotten so close, in some places in Indiana, they won't serve us pizza anymore.

—*White House Correspondents' Dinner, Washington, D.C., April 25, 2015*

• ◆ •

Six years into my presidency some people still say I'm arrogant, aloof, condescending. Some people are so dumb.

—*White House Correspondents' Dinner, Washington, D.C., April 25, 2015*

• ◆ •

People always ask me about Roswell and the aliens and UFOs, and it turns out the stuff going on that's top secret isn't nearly as exciting as you expect.

—*Interview, GQ, November 17, 2015*

• ◆ •

And then there's Ted Cruz. Ted had a tough week. He went to Indiana—Hoosier country—stood on a basketball court, and called the hoop a "basketball ring." What else is in his lexicon? Baseball sticks? Football hats? But sure, I'm the foreign one.

—*White House Correspondents' Dinner, Washington, D.C., April 30, 2016*

If I ran a third time, it'd be sorta like doing a third *Hangover* movie. It didn't really work out very well, did it?

 —*Interview with Zach Galifianakis,* Between Two Ferns, *March 11, 2014*

• ◆ •

But there is no doubt that Michael is a better golfer than I am. Of course if I was playing twice a day for the last fifteen years, then that might not be the case.

 —*Responding to basketball player Michael Jordan's quip that Obama is a bad golfer, radio interview, WJMR, Milwaukee, November 4, 2014*

• ◆ •

I would've enjoyed campaigning against Donald Trump. That would've been fun.

 —*Interview,* GQ, *November 17, 2015*

THE WISDOM OF
BARACK OBAMA

This is our first task—caring for our children. It's our first job. If we don't get that right, we don't get anything right. That's how, as a society, we will be judged.

—Interfaith prayer vigil after Sandy Hook school shootings,
Newtown, Connecticut, December 16, 2012

• ◆ •

Making your mark on the world is hard. If it were easy, everybody would do it. But it's not. It takes patience, it takes commitment, and it comes with plenty of failure along the way. The real test is not whether you avoid this failure, because you won't. It's whether you let it harden or shame you into inaction, or whether you learn from it; whether you choose to persevere.

—Campus Progress Annual Conference, Washington, D.C., July 12, 2006

• ◆ •

You have to go through life with more than just passion for change; you need a strategy. I'll repeat that. I want you to have passion, but you have to have a strategy. Not just awareness, but action. Not just hashtags, but votes.

—Commencement address, Howard University,
Washington, D.C., May 7, 2016

• ◆ •

We long for unity, but are unwilling to pay the price. But of course, true unity cannot be so easily won. It starts with a change in attitudes—a broadening of our minds, and a broadening of our hearts.

—Commemorating Martin Luther King Jr., Ebenezer
Baptist Church, Atlanta, January 20, 2008

And fear does funny things. Fear can lead us to lash out against those who are different, or lead us to try to get some sinister "other" under control. Alternatively, fear can lead us to succumb to despair, or paralysis, or cynicism. Fear can feed our most selfish impulses, and erode the bonds of community. It is a primal emotion—fear—one that we all experience. And it can be contagious, spreading through societies, and through nations. And if we let it consume us, the consequences of that fear can be worse than any outward threat.

—*National Prayer Breakfast, Washington, D.C., February 4, 2016*

Talk is cheap; like any value, empathy must be acted upon.

—The Audacity of Hope

Focusing your life solely on making a buck shows a poverty of ambition. It asks too little of yourself. And it will leave you unfulfilled.

—*Commencement address, Northwestern University, Evanston, Illinois, June 16, 2006*

Seek out people who don't agree with you. That will teach you to compromise. It will also help you, by the way, if you get married.

—*Town Hall with Young Leaders of the UK, London, April 23, 2016*

Participation in public life doesn't mean that you all have to run for public office—though we could certainly use some fresh faces in Washington. But it does mean that you should pay attention and contribute in any way that you can. Stay informed. Write letters, or make phone calls on behalf of an issue you care about.

—Commencement address, University of Michigan,
Ann Arbor, Michigan, May 1, 2010

• ◆ •

. . . [T]he arts are important. Artistic expression is important. . . . Music, poetry, representations of life as it is and how it should be—those are the things that inspire people. Life is a combination of very practical things, right? You got to eat, you got to work, you got to build roads and make sure that some dam isn't ruining a community. But it's also the spirit that we have inside of us, and how is that expressed, and what are our vision and what are our ideals for the future, and how do we want to live together, and how do we treat each other.

—Response to question, Young Southeast Asian Leaders Initiative
Town Hall, Ho Chi Minh City, Vietnam, May 25, 2016

• ◆ •

Being interested and engaged in life is the single most important pathway to success.

—Video interview with baseball player Derek Jeter,
The Players' Tribune, *June 22, 2016*

Wherever your hard work and talents take you—whether it's becoming a cardiovascular surgeon, the President of the United States, or chasing a dream you've yet to discover—always remember that you have a big role to play in shaping the world and making a difference in people's lives. Your enthusiasm and drive give me great hope for the future, and I am confident you can achieve your highest aspirations if you put your best effort into everything you do. I expect great things from you!

—Reply to letter from eight-year-old girl named Lily, August 3, 2016

CHRONOLOGY

August 4, 1961—Barack Obama Jr. is born in Honolulu, Hawaii. He is the son of Barack Obama Sr., a 25-year-old Kenyan student at the University of Hawaii, and (Stanley) Ann Dunham, an 18-year-old student born in Kansas, also at the University of Hawaii. Barack Obama Sr. had left Kenya in 1959 on a fellowship, leaving behind his pregnant wife (Kezia) and his son, Roy. Barack Obama Sr. and Ann Dunham married on February 2, 1961.

June 1962—Barack Obama Sr. is awarded a scholarship to Harvard University, and leaves to pursue his PhD in economics.

1964—Ann Dunham files for divorce from Obama. Obama Sr. moves back to Kenya.

1967—Ann Dunham moves with her son and second husband, Lolo Soetoro, to Indonesia.

1970—Barack's half sister Maya Soetoro is born. Barack (known as Barry) is nine years old.

1971—Barack returns to Hawaii to live with maternal grandparents, Stanley and Madelyn ("Toot") Dunham. He begins fifth grade at Punahou School.

1971—Barack Obama Sr. visits Hawaii for one month. Barack's mother returns to Hawaii during the visit.

1974—Ann separates from her second husband and returns to Hawaii. She resumes her studies at the University of Hawaii pursuing a graduate degree in anthropology.

1976—Ann returns to Indonesia for fieldwork in connection with her degree. Barack stays behind in Hawaii and continues living with his grandparents.

1979—Obama graduates from Punahou School. He moves to Los Angeles to attend Occidental College.

1981—Obama visits his mother and sister in Asia. He later moves to New York where he attends Columbia University.

November 24, 1982—Barack Obama Sr. dies in a car crash. Obama is twenty-one years old. He hadn't seen his father since the elder Obama's one and only trip to Hawaii.

1983—Graduates from Columbia with a degree in political science. He later visits his mother and sister in Indonesia.

1984 to 1985—Works in New York at the Business International Corporation and the New York Public Interest Research Group.

1985 to 1988—Moves to Chicago and begins working as a community organizer on the South Side of Chicago.

Summer 1988—Travels to Kenya to meet with and learn more about his family there.

September 1988—Enters Harvard Law School.

June 1989—Meets Michelle Robinson while working as a summer associate. She is a lawyer at the firm and his advisor. The two begin dating later in the summer.

February 1990—Elected the first African-American president of the *Harvard Law Review.*

June 1991—Graduates from Harvard Law School receiving his JD degree, magna cum laude.

1991—Returns to Chicago. He and Michelle Robinson get engaged.

October 18, 1992—Marries Michelle Robinson.

1992—Accepts position practicing civil rights law in Chicago law firm and teaches constitutional law at the University of Chicago Law School.

November 7, 1995—Obama's mother dies of cancer in Honolulu at the age of fifty-two.

1995—Obama publishes a memoir, *Dreams from My Father: A Story of Race and Inheritance.*

1996 to 2004—Wins election to Illinois State Senate. During his tenure, Obama passes substantial ethics reform, reduces taxes for working families, and expands health care.

1998—Daughter Malia is born.

March 2000—Runs against Bobby Rush in Democratic primary for Congress and loses the election.

2001—Daughter Natasha ("Sasha") is born.

July 2, 2004—Delivers the keynote address at the Democratic National Convention.

November 4, 2004—Wins his bid for U.S. Senate seat with the largest electoral victory in Illinois history. He is forty-two years old.

October 2006—Publishes his second book, *The Audacity of Hope: Thoughts on Reclaiming the American Dream.*

February 10, 2007—Announces his candidacy for president in Springfield, Illinois.

June 3, 2008—After a close battle with Hillary Clinton, Obama becomes the Democratic Party's presumptive nominee.

November 4, 2008—Defeats Republican John McCain and is elected as the 44th president of the United States and the first African-American president. Joe Biden becomes Vice President.

January 20, 2009—Sworn in as 44th president of the United States.

October 9, 2009—Awarded the Nobel Peace Prize.

January 27, 2010—Delivers first State of the Union Address.

March 23, 2010—Signs the Affordable Care Act into law.

July 21, 2010—Signs the Dodd-Frank Wall Street Reform and Consumer Protection Act into law.

December 22, 2010—Signs repeal of the "Don't Ask, Don't Tell" policy that banned openly gay people from serving in the military.

May 1, 2011—Announces in televised press conference that Osama bin Laden has been killed by U.S. forces in a raid in Pakistan.

May 25, 2011—Travels to Great Britain and addresses the UK Parliament, becoming the first U.S. president to do so.

October 21, 2011—Announces withdrawal of nearly all U.S. troops in Iraq by December 31, fulfilling his campaign promise to end the war.

June 2012—Supreme Court upholds the Affordable Care Act's individual mandate, which mandated citizens to purchase health insurance or pay a tax.

June 15, 2012—Issues executive order suspending deportation of class of young undocumented immigrants who'd arrived to the U.S. as children.

September 6, 2012—Accepts the Democratic nomination for president at the Democratic National Convention.

November 6, 2012—Wins reelection as president, beating Republican challenger Mitt Romney by close to 5 million votes.

December 14, 2012—School shooting at Sandy Hook Elementary School in Newtown, Connecticut, leaves twenty children and six adults dead. President Obama visits two days later and makes a pledge to fight for common-sense gun-control measures.

December 2012—Named *Time* Person of the Year for the second time. (He was also named *Time*'s Person of the Year in 2008.)

January 20, 2013—Is sworn in for his second term in a private ceremony in the White House. The inauguration is held on Martin Luther King, Jr. Day.

April 15, 2013—Terrorist bombing takes place at the Boston Marathon, killing three and leaving more than two hundred injured. Obama speaks at memorial service three days later.

April 2013—Obama's common-sense gun measures are blocked by Congress.

July 2013—Addresses the Trayvon Martin ruling after a Florida jury votes to acquit George Zimmerman in the murder of the African-American teen.

September 2013—Announces proposed plan made by Russia to Syrian leader Bashar al-Assad to relinquish Syria's chemical weapons in order to avoid military strikes.

September 2013—Speaks by telephone with Iranian president Hassan Rouhani, marking the first direct communication between the leaders of the respective countries in more than thirty years.

August 2014—Orders first air strikes against terrorist group known as ISIS or ISIL.

December 2014—Announces plan to normalize diplomatic relations with Cuba and relax economic restrictions with the island nation.

June 26, 2015—Supreme Court reverses a lower court decision to make same-sex marriage legal throughout the United States. In May 2012, Obama had voiced his support of same-sex marriage, the first president to do so.

June 2015—Speaks at the funeral of Reverend Clementa C. Pinckney, one of nine African-Americans killed by a white gunman who opened fire during a Bible study meeting at the Emanuel A.M.E. Church in Charleston, South Carolina.

July 2015—Announces the Iran Nuclear Deal, an agreement reached by the U.S. and five world powers aimed at limiting Iran's nuclear program.

July 23, 2015—Travels to Kenya, becoming the first American president to do so.

August 2015—Announces the Clean Power Plan in an effort to combat global climate change.

November 2015—Takes a lead role in the international COP21 summit held outside of Paris, which leads to the Paris Agreement, deemed by Obama as the "enduring framework" needed to solve the climate crisis.

January 2016—Announces series of executive orders to combat gun violence.

January 12, 2016—Delivers final State of the Union Address.

March 2016—Meets with Canadian Prime Minister Justin Trudeau in the first official visit from a Canadian leader in close to twenty years. Announces nominee Merrick Garland for the Supreme Court to fill the vacancy from the death of Antonin Scalia. Republicans refuse to hold hearings to consider the nominee.

March 20, 2016—Makes historic trip to Cuba, becoming the first sitting U.S. president to visit in eighty-eight years.

May 27, 2016—Visits Hiroshima, Japan, becoming the first sitting U.S. president to do so.

June 9, 2016—Endorses Hillary Clinton for president.

June 23, 2016—Supreme Court rules on Obama's executive actions on immigration, remands the case back to the lower court and blocks the programs.

August 26, 2016—Expands the Papahānaumokuākea Marine National Monument off the coast of Hawaii to over 580,000 square miles, making it the world's largest protected marine sanctuary.